500

Tips for
Academic
Librarians

500
Tips for Academic Librarians

Sally Brown
Head of Quality Enhancement, University of
Northumbria at Newcastle
Bill Downey
Subject and Site Librarian, Kingston University
Phil Race
Programme Director, Durham University
Certificate in Teaching in Higher Education

Library Association Publishing
London

© Sally Brown, Bill Downey, Phil Race 1997

Published by
Library Association Publishing
7 Ridgmount Street
London WC1E 7AE

Library Association Publishing is wholly owned by The Library Association.

First published 1997

British Library Cataloguing in Publication Data
A catalogue record for this book is available from the British Library.

ISBN 1-85604-228-6

Enquiry desk
027.7
BRO

Typeset in Castle and Century Oldstyle by Library Association Publishing.
Printed and made in Great Britain by Bookcraft (Bath) Ltd, Midsomer Norton, Avon.

Contents

Contents

Prologue

Academic librarians in forefront of information revolution – headline in The Times

Ah, good morning, I'm sorry to bother you.
   That's what we're here for. How can I help?
Well, I've just taken up a short-term contract here at Poppleton University and I rather wanted to get the hang of how this library works.
   Which library did you have in mind?
Well, erm, *this* library. The one I'm standing in.
   But this isn't a library.
It isn't?
   Oh no, this is the University Information Resources Centre.
What happened to the library?
   I can't really say. I'm pretty new here myself. But this is definitely the Information Resources Centre.
I see. Well, in that case perhaps you'd be good enough to tell me where I might find the Chief Librarian?
   You mean the managing director of data and information services?
I suppose I must. Does he have a desk in this building?
   A work station?
Of course.
   No, he mostly works from home and establishes interconnectivity by campus LAN.
Of course.
   Perhaps I could help? Is there any particular service which interests you? As you can see, on this floor we have 126 Unix work stations with full Netscape browser facilities for Web search.
I was really wanting something a shade more specific.

Prologue

Then perhaps you might like to take advantage of one of the two hundred work stations on the third floor which not only offer Z39.50 access protocol but also provide the opportunity for reading full-text E-journals with Adobe Acrobat.

Even more specific than that.

What exactly?

What I rather had in mind was borrowing a book.

Laurie Taylor
Reproduced with kind permission.

Foreword

Librarians are busy people. They spend most of their time looking after other people, usually in the confines of their own spaces, whether they are called libraries, learning resources centres, or something similar. Academic librarians are no exception to any of this, except perhaps that the world of academic libraries has changed even faster than has been the case in some of the other branches of the profession.

There are plenty of books and learning resources on librarianship, and many courses designed to accredit librarians. This book is not intended to be a substitute for any of these resources or courses, but rather to be a companion to them. In fact, we believe that librarians are so busy that there is a need for some short, sharp, practical pointers: tips in other words. These are exactly what we have tried to provide in this book. There are in fact well over 500 tips in this book (over 600 for anyone who's counting!), and we hope that because of this you will not mind us sometimes repeating the same fundamental messages in different contexts in the book, where the messages can be regarded as important. We have done this to help you get the most out of this book, not by reading it from cover to cover, but by dipping into it as and when you need it, and when you have time to make use of it.

Who is this book aimed at? We've tried to include everyone who works in libraries in universities and colleges, from managers to library assistants. This means, of course, that we don't expect every single tip to be relevant or useful to every single reader. Some tips are more aimed towards the managers of academic libraries, while others are aimed at everyone who works in them. Since there are more people who aren't managers, most of our suggestions are aimed at the people who actually do the bits and pieces which keep college libraries going. However, we hope that our book will be found valuable by those in control of such

Foreword

libraries, not least as an aid to their efforts to help their staff work effectively, productively, and happily in the many aspects of library work we have covered.

We started out by trying to write ten tips on each of over 50 aspects of academic librarians' work. It did not work out quite that way! In many cases, we thought of many more than ten, and the feedback we received on our pilot versions encouraged us not to stick to tens when there were many more suggestions we could make, but to include everything that may be of use to colleagues in college libraries. We therefore ended up with 39 headings, some of which have many more than ten suggestions under them.

How to use this book

We would not presume to tell librarians how to use books! However, we hope that you will find the book useful when used in one or more of the following ways:

- If you're new to library work, we hope you will find it a useful companion during your settling-in time.
- If you're an experienced hand at working in academic libraries, we hope you will find that our book gives you some ideas that you may not otherwise have thought of, and at least some confirmation of all the things you are doing well.
- If you're being trained for library work, we hope that our book will help you to construct a picture of the sorts of roles and duties that you may encounter when you enter the library profession.
- If you're a manager of an academic library, we hope that our book will help you to provide a frame of reference for your staff, upon which they can build to make your library function to everyone's satisfaction.

Sally Brown
Bill Downey
Phil Race

Acknowledgments

The authors are very grateful to participants at the Grasmere NATFHE Library Section Conference on 'Value for Money', who gave many useful suggestions for the improvement of the draft edition used at the Conference. In particular, we thank: Biddy Fisher, Scott Robertson, Chris Kelland, Charlotte Everitt, Ian Radcliffe, Sue Fellows, Marlene Godfrey, John Newton-Davies, Richard Harvey and Beth Jones, and other conference participants who may not have supplied their names with their feedback.

We are also very grateful to Robert Bluck of the University of Northumbria at Newcastle, who provided deep and helpful feedback which caused us to revise and improve many of the suggestions in this book. We would also like to thank Helen Ward of Kingston University for her many helpful suggestions.

Finally, we thank Helen Carley of Library Association Publishing not only for her encouragement as we worked towards the completion of this book, but for really useful feedback about things we had missed, and various aspects of the way we had addressed some of the things we had covered.

Chapter 1
Library matters

It was not easy for us to decide how best to try to start this book. We gradually found that there were several aspects of librarianship that did not fit under 'supporting students' or 'supporting academic staff' or 'looking after yourself', but were about the nature and ethos of the roles of librarians.

We start the book with 'The nature of library work', which is more a statement of the status quo of the position that librarians find themselves in, than a collection of suggestions to make to colleagues in libraries. We attempt then to get the balance right by moving on to 'Keeping on top of the job' with some general, practical suggestions regarding how to handle some of the most basic and fundamental aspects of being a librarian. Many of these suggestions are expanded upon in later sections of our book.

We move next to the big picture: institutional politics. Life would indeed be nice if such matters had no place in a book such as this. However, the real world of educational institutions is far from apolitical, so we have tried to muster our collective experience of such matters to offer some practical advice for librarians on how to find out more about such politics, and how to tune in to them.

Next, we address 'Motivating library staff'. We have all seen evidence of demotivation. Library staff, working in service provision, often seem to be subjected to the whims and beliefs of the various categories of people served by their libraries, and to an extent where the level of motivation they bring to their work can be impaired. Our suggestions offer some ways of getting over this problem.

We end this chapter with some suggestions on 'Working with computers'. We must say at once that we hope that these suggestions are not taken in the wrong spirit, as we have learned more about computers ourselves from library colleagues than from anyone else. Also, with many institutions moving towards converged library and computing services, the likelihood of there being expert computing skills to hand in the library is increased. The information technology explosion has affected few places more than libraries, and our suggestions are primarily aimed at colleagues who have little experience of computers, and should be skipped by the many readers of this book who will know much more about such devices than the three authors collectively!

1 The nature of library work

What is the essence of working in a modern library? The following ten dimensions give just an outline of some of the factors which may be involved in your job, and how librarians approach some of the aspects of their work.

1. **For many librarians, the interruptions are the job.** Library work is, and always will be, oriented towards people. The people served are the important part of the job, and this overrides the importance of any of the particular processes librarians are involved in. So if you're working anywhere where users can talk to you, don't expect to get your head down for too long: when you're being interrupted you're probably doing your job.

2. **Librarians mostly tend to be cooperators.** This is a strength when working in teams, which librarians tend to do very well. but there is a down side too. As a group librarians tend not to question why they are doing something, but to accept it at face value. Lemmings are cooperative too! A consequence of being too cooperative is that librarians sometimes have a sense of being an under-appreciated group. As a group, librarians feel that their role in institutions could be improved by a higher public profile. The key roles librarians can play in optimizing teaching quality assessments is tending to promote a better profile.

3. **But some librarians have territorial tendencies!** This can cause problems in the sort of service they aim to provide. There is little real payoff associated with empire-building in libraries. Librarians are as good at making themselves exclusive and isolated as most other professionals. Whenever a

group of librarians gets together, a forest of acronyms often grows.

4. **Librarians like to say 'yes'!** They are not in a backroom kind of job, even though they are often perceived as being in background roles. Working with students and academics, there is a tendency for librarians to become conditioned almost to say 'yes' all the time. They like to be able to say 'yes, we've got a really good collection of books and other resources on whatever-it-is'. It is also important to be able to say 'no', such as 'Sorry, but this won't be back in stock till next Wednesday'.

5. **What is important to librarians is not always what is important to others.** For some librarians it may be a bitter pill to swallow that almost nobody cares about the actual classification system they use or the quality of their cataloguing. What users want to know is: 'have you got it?', 'where is it please?' and 'why can't I find it then?' or 'how long can I have it for?'.

6. **Librarians are often 'pig in the middle'.** As theirs is a user-centred profession, it is important that they are seen to be sympathetic to users, even when it is not possible to do what they would like, because, for example, of budget constraints.

7. **Librarians' jobs are about meeting information needs.** Their most important jobs are a mixture of sorting out what the information needs of their institutions are, and meeting the individual information needs of users. However, nobody will tell you what the overall institutional information needs actually are – you have to go out and discover them for yourself, and piece together the jigsaw of information as best you can. Doing this helps the library to be seen as being pro-

active, and you build links between the library and schools or departments.

8. **There is necessarily some tension between effective liaison, and meeting day-to-day demands.** This is a difficult balance to get right. Liaison is the easier part to tackle, since it is more effective the more effort is put into it. But the more time you put into it, the more work you make for yourself, while at the same time having to keep the bread-and-butter services going.

9. **There is a similarity between library work and warehousing.** Librarians are responsible for storing and arranging large quantities of products, in many different formats and varieties. There's heavy work such as humping around heavy loads, unloading lorries, and even moving entire libraries. Librarians are, however, also responsible for knowing what these products are, what they are good for, and how best to use them. The different kinds of demands can change by the minute. The job therefore is a mixture of the cerebral and the practical, and requires quick change acts.

10. **There are almost certainly no perfect solutions to librarians' major problems.** Librarians are at the cutting edge of the information revolution (and always have been even before anyone noticed one). This means that their work will continue to involve devising better systems for meeting the needs of users, within the resources available, and within whatever accommodation can be acquired for this purpose. Librarians must also accept that as improvements are effected, expectations rise further. They can never guarantee to make all of their users happy (though it is reputed that students regard library heaven as unlimited, queue-free, free photocopying, and their very own networked PC).

11. **Librarians are at the sharp edge of technology.** Libraries still contain lots of books, journals and papers, but once these formats were the sharp edge of technology too. Now, information is increasingly computer-based and electronic, alongside the hard copy on the shelves. Electronic journals and networked provision to other libraries in franchise-linked institutions bring new demands on librarians. This means that many (but not all) librarians need to be technologists as well as everything else we have mentioned. Many indeed excel in this new role, and indeed are at the forefront of working with both students and academic staff in helping to promote computer-literacy, electronic communication, and computer-aided information retrieval skills.

2 Keeping on top of the job

A librarian's work can be varied, unpredictable and difficult to plan, as is often the case with a user-centred profession. These tips are designed to help you keep on top of the work in a flexible and responsive way.

1. **Train yourself to be relaxed about interruptions.** It can be frustrating, when you are working in the public eye, not to be able to get your head down to a task. It is human nature to feel irritated at being interrupted, but for some parts of your work this is going to be inevitable. When you are timetabled on a service point, try to find some job that is suitable for you to pick up between interruptions. Accept that service points hardly ever bring a constant flow of work. Find a task that will stand frequent interruption because it is not important if it does not get finished at the time, but which will help the time to pass more productively and quickly if things are quiet.

2. **Tell users how to do things, rather than always doing it for them.** There are times when you need to show people how to do things, but people learn things much better when someone talks them through doing it for themselves. In the long run, helping your users to be more self-sufficient makes them more satisfied too.

3. **Become skilled at finding out what people really want.** When users make a clumsy enquiry, it is not that they are trying to be difficult, but more likely that they don't know how exactly to put what they want into the right words. Becoming good at second-guessing what they really want is a help to all concerned. 'Would it be useful if I were to show you how to . . . ?' can be a useful approach to getting down to what they are really looking for help on.

4. **Don't expect information technology always to be the answer.** IT solves many problems, but can also bring its own trials and tribulations, until new systems are working smoothly. Expect the frustrations that go with incomplete operations manuals, incorrectly installed software, and insufficient training. All of these are temporary problems, and don't mean that the technology will never work well.

5. **Aim to be able to do running repairs.** A great deal of time is now spent servicing or keeping pieces of equipment operational, including photocopiers, printers, binding machines, language laboratory machines and all kinds of computer-based equipment. The situation is helped when all staff are *au fait* with the basic problems which tend to re-occur, such as paper jams, changing printer cartridges, and so on. It also helps if everyone knows when, and how, to call out the engineers. It is useful to log calls to engineers in an agreed place, so that anyone can direct the engineer on arrival to the source of the trouble. Such logs are useful evidence should there be any dispute regarding whether or when an engineer arrived after a call.

6. **Be willing to learn from students.** Especially when it comes to computers, when one machine is not working properly, the student who is already working on the next machine may be as good as anyone at knowing what to try. Students, like anyone else, like to feel valued for their particular skills, and as long as you enlist their help in the right way they are usually only too willing to help.

7. **Don't go it alone.** Librarians tend to work well in teams. Use the people you work with as a resource to help you make your job manageable, and be prepared to be a good team player when others are in need of a helping hand. Ideally, all staff should be able to do most library tasks and to cover for colleagues who are off sick, or who are hard-pressed. This is

easier to achieve in a small library where there is usually a 'Jack of all trades' culture anyway.

8. **Accept that there will always be unfinished business.** It would be strange if there were to be a time when there were no jobs waiting to be done – indeed that would probably be more stressful than the usual position.

9. **Distinguish between the urgent and the important.** Some things can be quite urgent, but not really important, and sometimes it is wise to make sure that the important things are getting enough of your attention. It can be a useful strategy to do one important (but not too time consuming) task *before* getting down to an urgent task. The urgent one will probably get done anyway, and be none the worse for being that little bit later.

10. **Find out as much as you can about what everyone else can do well.** In a customer service setting, it's not possible for any one person to have all the answers. However, it is almost always possible to 'know someone who does'.

11. **Be alert for new ideas.** Keep on top of your job by reading professional journals, keeping up with your specialisms, and volunteering for training in new fields. All major organizations regard continuous change as a perpetual state of being. Try to ensure that you are as prepared as anyone for what's just around the corner.

12. **Keep staff training in mind all the time.** The best ideas for staff training concern the things that staff really need to be able to do or to know about, and such ideas almost always crop up during normal working days rather than when someone sits down to think about training needs.

3 Getting to grips with your institution's politics

It is useful, indeed necessary, to understand the politics in your own library, and the related politics in schools, faculties, and across the institution as a whole. If you are new, this is often one of the most difficult aspects of the job to tune in to: some of the politics will be shrouded in history, and people may be unwilling to tell you about it. Every institution is different, and yours may seem baffling in its complexity when you first start working in it. The following tips may help you to map out the terrain and to start to understand how your university or college works.

1. **Read the paperwork.** Get hold of the key policy documents, mission statement, institutional and departmental plans and familiarize yourself with the contents. Don't feel you have to read every word unless you are an insomniac: use the executive summaries as far as you can.

2. **Find out about the TLAs (and others).** Universities and colleges are rife with Three Letter Acronyms (and longer ones). You can feel rather foolish if you don't know that a DRD is a Definitive Route Document or whatever the acronym might be. Make yourself a little glossary (and you may find established staff are asking you for a copy of it!).

3. **Find out about the hierarchies.** There will probably be diagrams representing the workings of the upper echelons, but it is a good idea to ask someone to explain to you the workings of the lower reaches of your institution.

4. **Familiarize yourself with the key people.** These are not necessarily the most senior people, (although you will need to put names to the faces of these people) but are those who

have key functions within the organization. You may learn a lot from a junior assistant to a university or college senior manager, who may have more time to put you in the picture.

5. **Look out for the 'kitchen cabinet'.** In most institutions, and sections of an institution, there is usually such a group, where the key decisions are really made. Such groups often meet informally, but get their key players involved in working parties and sub-committees.

6. **Observe how people behave in meetings.** It is sometimes surprising how people change when they get into a room full of their own colleagues. Watch who does the talking, who does the organizing, and who makes sure that business is pushed through. Watch also who does the distracting, and who does not seem to contribute. Observe how decisions are reached in meetings, and who seems to be most able to secure a decision.

7. **Find out about the committee structure.** It may help to make yourself an overview in diagrammatic form if this doesn't exist somewhere in the documentation so you can see how the different committees relate to one another.

8. **Go back to the future.** For any committee in which you are involved, obtain the minutes of several previous meetings and read your way into the context. Doing this will help to stop you feeling out of your depth at your first meeting.

9. **Get yourself a mentor.** Find someone who has been around the place for several years who isn't too cynical (not always an easy task!) and ask them to explain the way the place works. If in doubt about something in particular, check out what other people feel, until you've built up a balanced picture of the prevailing views.

10. **Get the low down on the past.** Finding out who doesn't get on with who and who are good friends with each other will help you avoid putting your foot in it with tactless observations. Universities and colleges are just villages really when it comes to interpersonal relationships, and old feuds and loyalties die hard.

11. **Don't become a maverick.** If you're involved in getting changes and developments approved in the institution, make sure that everything goes through the appropriate pathways or committees, and that the proposals or ideas you are putting in are clearly documented in minutes or supporting papers.

12. **Be in all the right places at all the right times.** Collaborate with your colleagues so that the library perspective pervades as many as possible of the relevant decision-making processes and forums in your institution. Make time for colleagues to exchange news of what they've found is going on in different areas of the institution.

13. **Be ready to inform policy decisions.** Don't jump in too early with suggestions, but discuss developments with your own colleagues, and agree on the directions that you collectively wish to aid and abet. Then feed in appropriate recommendations to decision-making groups, with an eye to the way you wish to see strategic planning developing.

14. **If unsure, ask.** Ask the right person at the right time, however, rather than give the impression that 'someone from the Library didn't even know that...' to people.

4 Motivating library staff

Sometimes library staff appear to be demotivated! There are all sorts of reasons for this. Indeed, teaching staff in many institutions are also much more stressed and demotivated than they have ever felt before, they say! Demotivation can be attributed to all sorts of causes, and usually managers get the blame. Library work involves staff working together effectively, so motivation becomes crucial. The following suggestions may help bring the problems surrounding motivation to the surface, when many of them can be tackled. Some of these suggestions are aimed at managers, but all of them work best when everyone tries to put them into practice.

1. **Feel good about being a librarian!** Avoid the sort of sentence-starter: 'Well, I'm only a librarian, but I think that....'. This sort of opening often happens when librarians are attending meetings or committees outside the library. People's motivation is increased when they feel respected, so don't put yourself down.

2. **Don't blame the boss.** We can all remember working for better bosses than our current one. Or was it that times were easier in the past, and the boss's work was happier? It takes more than one person so make – or to break – the motivation of a group of people working in a library. In any case, a really bad boss can motivate a team to work together despite such a person, as strongly as a really good boss can create positive motivation.

3. **Don't blame the government.** When there is any kind of stress, turbulence, or change, it is human nature to want to find someone to blame. It does not solve the problems, how-

ever, and adds to the given impression of being a demotivated team.

4. **Don't blame one another.** There may well be things wrong with the workings of various members of the team, but just blaming someone does not usually cause them to act any better. People usually know when they aren't pulling their weight, or when their work is not being particularly successful.

5. **Don't blame yourself either!** There seems to be a sort of misplaced acceptance-of-blame tendency prevalent in many librarians. It's not all your fault, whatever it is. The most that can be asked of your work with students, academics and each other is about making things better, not perfect.

6. **Try to be aware of when you are moaning!** Everyone grumbles at times of course, but people can sometimes forget that they are doing it, until it spreads like an infectious disease. It can become a habit, and it is depressing for anyone who becomes surrounded by people doing it. So check whether you are spreading the disease.

7. **If you are the boss, tackle the problem of motivation head on.** Staff working in libraries are not brilliantly paid, and normally respond positively to encouragement and being valued. Don't take their motivation for granted. It is so much better for them to go to work feeling well motivated and purposeful than cynical or depressed, and you can work at achieving a better feeling about their work with them.

8. **Notice what staff are doing and always comment when something is done well.** Praise motivates, so why does it seem to be given so seldom? Reticence, shyness and fear of embarrassment on the part of the librarian certainly play a part but the major reason is that too often we do not notice. Some librarians take the attitude that if things are done well

then there is nothing to complain about. This means that only the negative aspects of staff performance are likely to be noted, and not the positive actions.

9. **Praise has to be genuine.** For praise to be genuine you first have to notice good performance and secondly recognize it as such. Most staff know how well they are performing at any one time. If they know they can do a job either well or badly without anybody in authority noticing or caring, there is less incentive to do it well. There is nothing worse or more obvious than insincere praise, and it simply discredits the person giving it and devalues the person receiving it.

10. **Work out a number of different ways of saying 'well done'.** Praising a member of staff will probably be embarrassing if it is done with an anodyne stock phrase. It does not have to be effusive, condescending or a formal pat on the head. It works best by simply letting someone know you have noticed what they have done well and should ideally spring from a natural situation. Here are some basic examples. A member of staff sorts out a collection which was in a mess: 'Well, you've knocked that into shape'. A new display: 'That looks nice'. A long and tedious job is finished: 'Thanks for battling your way through that'. Such praise can be genuinely motivating. Try to think of a number of different ways of saying 'well done'.

11. **Start looking for what is being well done.** When we are all too busy we tend to notice the things that go wrong, rather than the things that work well. In any service, the emphasis tends to be on dealing with complaints, rather than coping with praise. Change this emphasis within your team, and you may be surprised at how much is going well.

12. **Open a 'thanks!' box.** There is probably already a suggestions box or a complaints procedure for users who are not

satisfied with the service or provision in the library. Opening a 'thanks' box can elicit some gestures of appreciation from users too. One reason why librarians may not get too many votes of thanks is because people don't really know how to go about it, and may be embarrassed to approach individuals personally to do so.

13. **Small actions also count.** Look for the little, but useful, things that people do which are not specifically in their job description. Which members of staff move calendar dates on, water the plants, tidy counters at the end of the day, do the tea fund, or clean terminal screens? In other words who pays attention to small tasks which oil the wheels and keep the show running smoothly? These are the little things which it is so easy to take for granted but which are so annoying if nobody takes responsibility for them.

14. **Criticism is not the same as blaming.** You can criticize an action, or a process, without blaming the person involved directly. It is far easier for any of us to change some of our actions or some of the processes we use, than to change ourselves as people. Therefore having our actions criticized should not be felt in the demotivating way that we might feel if we were criticized as people.

15. **Talk to your people.** Try to have a few words with each of those members of staff under your direct supervision every day. There is often a feeling among staff that managers are not interested in them as people, and this is frequently not without foundation. In concentrating on getting tasks done and achieving goals, it is all too easy to forget that your staff are people and that the library is not their whole life.

16. **Be willing to listen.** Without being intrusive, you need to be willing to get to know them as people and they need to feel that they can talk to you. If you are approachable and pro-

vide a sympathetic ear, staff are more likely to tell you of problems they may have – and will appreciate the fact that you are willing to listen. This will not happen if you don't make the effort to talk to them or regard it simply as a waste of time.

17. **Within sensible limits, let staff re-design their own jobs.** This needs of course to be done bearing in mind job descriptions, salaries and grades: we can't just let everyone design out of their job the bits they don't like! That said, when staff have been in particular posts for a few months, they may well have ideas about how their work could be done better. It is important to tap into this knowledge and let staff test-fly their own kites. Most staff welcome the opportunity to put their own ideas into practice. It creates a feeling of job ownership, and shows that you are willing to trust them.

18. **Encourage ownership of decisions.** Virtually all members of staff want more involvement in what they do but it is very easy to kill off this spirit of enterprise. In staff meetings you can brainstorm possible solutions to problems and then ask staff to prioritize the ideas. When the staff come up with the solutions to problems themselves, there is likely to be a much greater feeling of ownership of them. It is much better than one person dictating what shall be done.

19. **Try to avoid an atmosphere where everyone takes everything far too seriously.** A little humour can go a long way with most people. Staff enjoying themselves at work is a good sign, not a bad one! Don't make humour mandatory, though. Use it only when it works, and when no-one feels offended or discomforted by it.

20. **Allow people to be honest without fear of recrimination.** At the end of the day, staff feel happiest working in an environment where honest communication is possible. An

atmosphere of forced 'niceness' where no-one expresses what they really think is a pretty sure sign that people feel threatened by anyone who may disagree with them. Such an atmosphere is unsuccessful at fostering real motivation.

21. **Remember that money is not the only motivator.** People work for many other reasons than the financial. Responsibility, status, respect, self development – even enjoyment – are all words that spring to mind. It is not always in our power to offer financial incentives, but it is always worth remembering that there are other possible incentives open to us.

22. **Have a short 'accolades' round to start off staff meetings.** Ask everyone to give one positive comment about something that someone else has done last week. Maybe set the groundrule that the accolades reported in the round must have no victim! (This may avoid problems of the sort where someone reports something like the action of the person who accidentally rammed the Vice-Chancellor's car in the car park!).

5 Working with computers

Gone are the days when books and papers were the only contents of libraries. Library staff and library users alike make more use of computer-based systems every day. It can be somewhat traumatic making one's first encounters with such technologies; we hope the following suggestions will help you to minimize such difficulties.

1. **Don't be blinded by science when someone demonstrates a new piece of equipment to you.** It's easy to get discouraged and feel 'I'll never remember all these things at once.' Don't even expect to learn how to use something from a demonstration of someone else using it: expect only to learn a bit about what it does and how it works.

2. **Learning is by doing – and making mistakes.** The best way to get started with a new machine or a new program is to try using it. It usually doesn't matter too much whether you use it correctly right from the start, so build in some informal practice until you feel ready to take the plunge.

3. **Don't be afraid to ask.** There's always someone who has already got the hang of a new computer-based package (and if you're that someone you don't need this set of tips!). Ask such a person to 'talk me through getting the thing to do so-and-so please' and make sure they make *you* do it rather than show you how they would do it.

4. **Be willing to keep up with technology.** The rate of development of computer-based technologies continues to accelerate. However competent you are with the things around you at the moment, give yourself time to check up what's coming on line, and keep yourself at the forefront of developments.

5. **Don't underestimate students.** While some students will need all the help they can get from you to get tuned in to computer-based packages in the library, there will always be some students who seem to have been born with modems instead of ears. Such students can help less-experienced users, and can often teach us a thing or two too.

6. **Keep backup copies of everything.** With academics, students and library staff using some machines, there is always the chance that software gets deleted or corrupted. There is also the possibility that alien software can get onto machines, and sometimes you may need to start with a blank hard disk again. Keep records of exactly what software is meant to be on which machine for such occasions.

7. **Keep your back-up disks somewhere else.** We know of one awful situation where a computer was stolen, together with all the back up disks which were in a locked box next to the machine! A fireproof safe for important resources may seem unduly neurotic, but such precautions are expected by insurance companies, so use them if they are available to you.

8. **Don't always assume it's your fault when the system crashes.** It's more than likely that it's nothing to do with you, even though you may be in the front line as far as people who are inconvenienced are concerned.

9. **Don't be afraid to use the help line.** You've probably already paid for such help when the software or hardware was purchased. Also, the cause may be a common problem, with a readily available solution at the end of the phone. Few problems are a global 'first'!

10. **Keep a regular log of breakdowns, faults, bugs and so on.** This helps to put them into perspective. Any problem may seem like a disaster at the time, but it's more important

to find out about the recurrent problems, so that decisions can be made regarding avoiding or overcoming them.

11. **Keep your files organized.** Remember to delete unnecessary or out-of-date ones. It's worth thinking about setting yourself a slot every week where you do such housekeeping operations with your information. The time you may otherwise waste, looking for a particular file among a mass of redundant information, justifies such housekeeping.

12. **Remember to include a footer including the file name.** This may seem simple, but it can save hours of searching and trying to remember what you called a particular file.

13. **Keep your own personal 'idiot's file'.** If you keep forgetting commands and actions, write them down for yourself and keep them handy. This will be more use than having to plough through the instruction book every time.

14. **Think about your health and safety.** If you are using a computer several hours a day, it's important that you use equipment that is ergonomically appropriate, with an anti-reflective screen on the monitor. Your institution should be looking after this for you, but if they don't, make a fuss until they do.

15. **Keep a written wish-list going.** You never know when you may have the chance to spend an unexpected bit of a budget. Knowing what you could usefully order, at a moment's notice, may bring some wishes to reality.

Chapter 2
Managing matters

Our next chapter collects together some suggestions relating to some of the diverse things that librarians manage. We start with the obvious one: 'Managing stock'. It is not surprising that we thought of nearly 30 suggestions on this topic alone. However, from these suggestions spring some of the more financial aspects of the work of librarians, and our next three sets of suggestions respectively look at 'Managing the journals budget', 'Managing the budget for your school, department or faculty' and 'Writing a business plan'. All of these sets embrace the problems of balancing financial matters with the business of providing the sort of service that our users require. We are aware, however, that with the increasing tendency for budgets to be devolved in institutions, readers may well not have as much control of some of these aspects of financial management than they might wish to have, and will need to adapt our suggestions to accommodate the specific financial circumstances that operate in their own institutions.

We move next to the other main aspect of management that librarians undertake, that of managing the use of the space for which they are responsible. In 'Managing library environments' we turn our attention to some suggestions for making the library as attractive as possible to the various kinds of users for whom it is intended to provide a service.

We end this chapter with another environmental issue, that of noise. Historically, this issue is a problematic one, in that libraries came to be considered as quiet places where people could read in virtual silence. Nowadays, in academic libraries, this history has to be balanced against the increasing realization that people learn a great deal when they actually talk to one another, particularly when looking together at the various kinds of learning resources that our libraries contain. In short, there are likely to remain two principal kinds of need: those of the people who wish to refer to learning resources privately and in conditions which enable them to concentrate as individuals, and those of the people who wish to come into libraries to work collaboratively and to learn by talking to one another about the things that they learn from the stock. We hope that the suggestions we offer will help both categories of users to find what they need in libraries.

6 Managing stock

It is an obvious but important point that librarians are in business only for so long as they have the stock that their users want to read, in the right quantities, and in the right places for them to find. The following suggestions may help you take stock of your stock position.

1. **Remember whom the stock is for.** In modern libraries, the stock has to serve the needs of larger groups of students than ever before, who are buying fewer textbooks of their own as the funding of higher education is increasingly being passed back to the customers. Students nowadays are more assertive, and better-aware of their rights, so libraries need to be seen to doing everything possible to make the most of limited resources.

2. **Be objective about stock complaints.** The main complaints about library services tend to be about the stock: that the libraries do not have the right books, or enough copies of the right books, or that the OPAC says the book is not on loan but it is not on the shelves. Some of this is of course outside librarians' control – lack of resources and so on – but too often the resources argument is used to cloak the fact that no work has been done on the existing stock.

3. **Be honest about the rubbish.** A lot of libraries are full of outdated stock which is not being read, will never be read, looks appalling and is stopping users from finding the 'live' stock hidden within its depths. It is vital that the stock is 'live' and also looks as good as possible.

4. **Remember that rubbish and valuable stock are two ends of a long scale.** Most books will travel along this scale

during their lifetime, some much faster than others. Essentially, the usage statistics are your best indicator regarding where any book is on its journey.

5. **Don't expect a book to be valuable just because *you* think it is valuable, or because it is included in other libraries that you know.** The actual demand on books is influenced quite a lot by the recommendations that are made by academic staff, and whether particular books are cited as relevant to particular student assignments and projects. Different books will be cited as valuable by academics in each institution. Therefore, try to tune in where possible to the likely nature of the demand for each book.

6. **Be ready to argue the case for multiple copies of set texts.** When prospective students are being shown around institutions, a selling-point for courses is often that the students don't have to buy many expensive textbooks.

7. **Work right through the stock at least once a year.** The summer holiday can be a good time to go through the areas you are responsible for and withdraw, relegate, update, change loan status – whatever has to be done. However, it is better to have a continuous stock reviewing policy. If sections have not been looked at for many years then it will be slow and painstaking work, but it does get easier after you have done it once.

8. **Don't just change everything during the summer!** Though there is more opportunity to make major changes when usage-levels are low, returning students and staff don't like to find everything in different places when they return. When a major change is necessary over a summer, run an appropriate help-desk for a while, and make leaflets summarizing the changes.

9. **Have a policy to weed the rubbish continuously.** This will be anathema to some, and a relief to many others; most librarians are running working libraries and not archives. Stock that has no value will vary from subject to subject – computing stock may only have a shelf life of five years whereas humanities stock lasts much longer – but if you look for rubbish in any area you will find it. Starting the processes to throw it away will create space, make your shelves look better, and probably put your loan statistics up.

10. **Remember the cataloguing implications.** This is another reason for avoiding major culls at any one time. It is important to keep each kind of catalogue up to date with the actual stock position, including any half-way positions where books shortly to be withdrawn entirely can still be obtained from a warehouse. Keep catalogues abreast of stock changes: computerization makes this much simpler.

11. **Have a clear policy on explaining and justifying what you throw out.** When you ask for permission to throw stock out there will be some academics who will suddenly find all sorts of reasons why you shouldn't. Some academics will still recommend textbooks from the '50s and '60s, may be explaining that 'these are seminal works which have never been bettered in 30 years and are just as applicable today' – possibly because they were what they used when they were studying.

12. **Consult academic staff appropriately.** If a book has not been used for some years, you've got your argument for withdrawing it. If staff protest at this possibility, find out which alternative books they may suggest that you could withdraw, and check their usage. Withdrawing without any consultation undermines liaison with academic staff and enrages them!

13. **Think where you'll send the old stock.** It may have to be disposed of entirely, but some of it could be of value to other libraries, or the Third World, or worth storing in an off-campus warehouse for a year before final disposal.

14. **Review your collections.** Too many special collections or special sequences just confuse users, who tend not to find in them the material they actually need. So as part of your stock reviewing process see if you can reintegrate any that have passed their sell-by date back into the main sequence. This is not to say that special collections do not have a value – just that they should be kept to a minimum.

15. **Have a policy on stock locations.** Don't just put them where some academics from the most relevant department suggest. There has to be an overall coherent policy so that everyone can see the logic of the stock arrangements.

16. **Make the loan system simple to understand.** When there are different categories of stock and different loan arrangements pertaining to special categories, it becomes important that users know exactly what they can borrow, for how long, and how many such loans they can make at once. If there are too many exceptions, confusion prevails.

17. **Stock should be 'ordinary lending' unless there is a very good reason for it not to be.** Whatever your other categories of stock are, make as much of it ordinary lending as possible. Students and staff tend to want to take out as much material as they can for the maximum permitted period. If a weekly loan book is not going out at least once a week for some weeks of the year at least, it should not be a weekly loan. Short loan arrangements need to be firmly based on demand patterns for the books involved.

18. **Have special arrangements for books that are in heavy demand for just a few weeks of each year.** Computerized

records show up such trends easily, and it is actually helpful to students to know that a particular book is going to be in heavy demand later in the year, and this encourages them to regard the book as more useful, and to make use of it earlier.

19. **Prune closed access collections regularly.** This is particularly relevant to short loan collections which cannot be browsed. If an item is not being used at least twice a week for at least part of the year, it probably has no business in a short loan collection. So much valuable stock is locked away in short loan collections and is not found by students and so is wasted. It is very important that you make the best use of what you have got.

20. **Keep reference material to a minimum.** The problem with reference material – particularly reference copies of recommended reading – is that they tend to be the books that are either hidden, stolen or vandalized. It is a sad fact that if a book can't legitimately be taken out when it is wanted, frustration is vented.

21. **Keep your stock control flexible.** It is very important that you should be able to transfer an item from one category of stock to another quickly and easily, and at any time of the year when demand justifies this. Computer systems make changing the catalogue easy but the books themselves should still not have to sit around waiting for labels to be changed.

22. **Be choosy about donations.** While in times of diminishing resources it is attractive to get anything free, books have no value in a library unless they are of interest and relevance to at least some readers. It is still sometimes worth accepting an entire collection for those books that will be of value, and regarding the task of disposing of the rest as a way of helping the donor.

23. **Classify new stock at locations where users are likely to look for them.** Most libraries have short-term display arrangements for important new stock, but many users will not see these displays regularly enough to keep track of what has gone into the system. Many users tend to have two or three places where they browse, and they tend not to extend their range much beyond these. Don't hide material from potential readers just because of the niceties of the classification system.

24. **Deal appropriately with 'shelf-ready' stock.** There is an increasing move towards stock which has already been classified when it comes into the library, and it is important to see whether this pre-classification fits in well with the existing arrangements for older stock.

25. **Make the fines system clear and workable.** If the system is clear and straightforward, it will reduce the time spent in arguments at the issue counter. It can be really useful to remind students of the relative loan arrangements of different books they are borrowing, for example 'these two are out to you for a month, but this one is due back next week, and is 50 pence a day if it is late'. Such conversations get over the 'I didn't realize this' or 'no-one told me about this' problems. Similarly, have arrangements for the minority of users who ignore overdue notices, such as temporarily withdrawing their borrowing rights until their records are put straight.

26. **Make statistics memorable.** Numbers mean little to most people, so saying the stock comprises 95000 volumes is of little significance. However, statements about stock along the following lines are more memorable: 'The stock returned on the first day of term weighed as much as a double-decker bus!' or '30% of the stock is now older than the average age of the new students!'.

7 Managing the journals budget

Unfortunately many college libraries don't have journal selection policies anymore, they have journal de-selection policies! With journal prices going up between 10% and 30% a year, and with level or decreasing funds, journal cuts are forced upon libraries. At the same time, in many subject areas, journals are the most under-used part of the library stock and therefore the least cost-effective. The following suggestions may make this area of work less traumatic.

1. **Put journals into perspective.** There is still the perception in some quarters that libraries are places where gold tooled volumes binding up every journal imaginable should line the shelves regardless of whether they are used or not. Usage statistics are, however, more complex than with stock. For example, if there is a small-but-successful research unit in for example interfacial electrochemical kinetics in your institution, keeping some expensive journals may be justified, but maybe the funding arising from the Research Assessment Exercise should play some part in acquiring these.

2. **Try to find out the perceived 'pecking order' of the journals in a field.** This changes with time, but colleagues in your institution who may have participated in Research Assessment Exercise processes (or had their own work involved in such processes) should be able to give librarians some feedback on which journals are deemed most important.

3. **Research the position elsewhere.** It can be useful to find out from colleagues in other institutions which journals are being cut. Bear in mind, of course, the different research interests involved.

4. **Maintain or reinstate a journal selection policy.** The fact that librarians won't often be able to order a new journal does not mean there should not be a policy for prioritizing and discussing everyone's claims and aspirations. The fact that a policy exists, and that only a small amount of money will be available, helps everyone understand the need for cutting other journals.

5. **Explain to staff that cuts will have to be made somewhere.** Academics tend to value the journal collection over and above the bookstock and if librarians ask them to recommend titles which should be cut, they will simply suggest others that they would like to be purchased. Impress upon them the need for cuts and because some many never have to deal with budgets, be patient when explaining the financial realities. With good reason, the necessity of making journal cuts is a nettle that many librarians fear to grasp.

6. **Students don't value journals so much.** While their lecturers might be happy about the fact that 90% of the school budget is spent on research journals, not many students will agree with them. This is one of the main areas where librarians may have to try to protect the students' interests.

7. **Have in mind a maximum amount that can be spent on journals.** This may be an actual sum of money or it may be a percentage of the overall budget for your school. If left unchecked the periodicals bill will progressively eat into other budgets until there is nothing left for anything else. So at a certain point alarm bells should definitely start ringing. Where this point is will depend on the nature of stock provision in the subject area. Once the estimated journal spend starts to exceed 50% of the school budget, then it may be a signal to start to worry.

8. **Try to get the maximum journal budget formalized.**
This is one of the possible uses of stockfund policy documents which are currently in vogue. If librarians can get it down in black and white that the school agrees to no more than $x\%$ of its money going on journals, then it may give useful leverage at a later date.

9. **Know which journals are used.** This is vital to know before any cutting exercise. Librarians can do surveys to get an accurate picture of what is being used and it is also useful to note which journals are cited in final year dissertations. However as users almost never reshelve their journals, keeping a mental note throughout the year of what is left out on the tables will tell you most of what they need to know, and is faster than most surveying methods! If a journal is always in order in its pamphlet box, then it is never used.

10. **Know which journals the students use.** This is not difficult as they tend to use very few. They also tend to be the inexpensive ones, so librarians may be able to defend keeping them. Very few journals that students regularly use cost more than £50 per year.

11. **Know why your library stocks the journals that it does.**
It is also important to know something of the history of each title and the reason it was acquired. A journal may be bought to support a particular academic's research. The research may change or the academic might leave. You may stock the expensive, multipart journal of a professional body, which is never used but which it would be unwise to cut as they accredit one of your courses.

12. **Prioritize each title.** In the 1980s librarians were encouraged to distinguish core titles from desirable titles. Many libraries are by now cutting well into the core which means

there is no alternative but to have a list of priorities for these titles.

13. **A decision to cut a title can always be reversed.** If librarians cut a title and there is an outcry, they can always reinstate it. No disaster has happened, and an apology may be all that is needed. What often happens when librarians cut a journal is that nobody notices, in which case money has been saved.

14. **Have consultation processes about journals to be cut.** To *have* such processes is the important thing; staff could be very critical if they thought that librarians were just making decisions without any reference to them.

15. **Know the criteria that will be used to make cuts.** This is your library's journal de-selection policy. Criteria for making cuts will be different in different situations. A major criterion will naturally be price but another is whether anyone will notice the absence of the journal.

16. **If possible, try not to broadcast the fact that cuts are being made.** As previously stated, if librarians proclaim to academics that they are making journal cuts – even of material which nobody ever looks at – academic staff will tend to find out reasons against making the cuts.

17. **Be ready to fight your case.** If there is an outcry about the decision to cut a particular journal, it can be very useful to enlist the help of someone from the school concerned whose say is taken seriously there, and it is useful to negotiate your proposed cuts informally with such key people in advance of making decisions.

18. **Keep track of journals that go directly to departments.** Sometimes academics may have their own personal subscriptions to journals (usually at a much lower cost than would be

charged to a library). Of course, it is not possible (or lawful!) then to expect them to make their copies available to anyone else, but such private collections can be a useful focus for reviewing whether to start or reinstate an institutional subscription. Also, many staff get copies of journals through acting as editors, reviewers or contributors.

19. **Consider collaboration with other local libraries.** Where there are several institutions in close geographic proximity, mutual collaboration can save each library from having to duplicate expensive or minority journals.

20. **Keep aware of which journals are now available electronically.** This can bring cost savings, not just in the actual subscription price, but in the overall cost of receiving, shelving, storing, and handling the journal. However, issues of computer equipment costs and availability which also need to be taken into account.

8 Managing the budget for your school, department or faculty

The suggestions in this section are only intended for readers who have a budget to control; if you have not got one, count your blessings. If, however, you are involved in the budget for books and journals of a school, department or faculty in your institution, we hope that you will find helpful these pragmatic suggestions regarding how to manage this money most appropriately.

1. **Always overspend rather than underspend.** Of course what librarians want to do is to bring the sections of the funds that they are responsible for home exactly on target. But remember that to underspend is the gravest of all crimes as the message it sends out to financial managers is that librarians will not need such a large allocation next year – so they won't get it. Overspending on the other hand gives out the message that although librarians have not managed the fund well, the school cannot survive on less. There are no prizes for financial prudence: the rule seems to be 'if you've got it, make sure you spend it'

2. **Give yourself room for manoeuvre in forecasting.** When you get your budget for the new financial year, you need to estimate the cost of your big recurrent items – periodicals, abstracts, CDs and so on – to give them the true picture of what they have got to spend. Allow more for inflation than might seem justified. This should give you more money than was thought to be available, rather than less.

3. **Keep tabs on the budget.** You will almost certainly get financial reports of how the spend for the year is progressing. Even so it is a good idea to keep a ready reckoner of what

you have committed and what you have spent. Then you have a clear idea of what the financial position is at any time and if any unexpected figures turn up in your financial reports – and they do have a tendency to – you are in a position to question them at an early date. It is particularly important towards the end of the financial year to know exactly what money you have left unspent.

4. **Commit your funds – or as much of the funds as you want to commit – well before the end of the financial year.** Despite electronic invoicing systems, the speed of return of ordered material from library suppliers is not fast and probably about 10% will not come back at all. The last thing that you want is for the end of the financial year to be approaching and there to be uncertainty as to whether a large batch of material you have ordered will arrive in time for your institution's cut-off date for invoices. It is best to allow several weeks for orders to be turned around – and to allow longer for orders from abroad.

5. **Never be unsure about anything to do with money.** If there are any financial figures that you don't understand or that don't seem right to you, question them at once. It costs nothing but a little time to seek clarification, but the amount you could save could be significant.

6. **Keep a wish list.** This could be a list of items that you would like to purchase if you had any extra money. Windfalls do occur once in a while but you usually have to spend the money quickly. A characteristic of higher education in the UK is that you have to scrimp and save for years on end, and this is followed by a brief, frenzied orgy of spending – which just occasionally spills over to libraries!

7. **Find a bookshop where you can buy off the shelf.** At the end of the financial year there is often still some money left

in the kitty, which needs to be spent quickly. If it is possible, try to find a specialist bookshop in your subject area where you can buy off the shelf and the goods can be delivered and invoiced within a week. Such places do still exist and have the added plus of staff who know their stock and can advise you on what is selling and what isn't.

8. **Get to understand how your institution's finance system works.** Most librarians don't need to go into this in detail, but it is useful for them to have a general understanding of how the institution divides up its money.

9. **Understand the working of your funding formula.** The money any library receives is divided up in some way: by number of students, by full time equivalents for example, or by historical allocation. It is important to understand the principles on which this division is based because academics may constantly ask you about it. They may want to know why their department or school receives less money for library spending than another. Librarians need to have a ready answer for this.

10. **Can you vire money from one budget to another?** You need to find out if you can do this and if so, what is the mechanism for doing it. If you can, it gives you more flexibility, and may allow schools or faculties to contribute to the fund should they so wish.

11. **Avoid being beholden.** Sometimes you can persuade your school or faculty to top up your stockfund, for example to purchase an expensive or prestige item. However, if this item is recurrent expenditure, you may have to go cap in hand next year, and the year after, and sooner or later they may say 'no'. Uncertainties in your financial position make budgets more difficult to manage.

12. **Try to keep the flow of spending going.** This can be diffi-
    cult, and you may have to work quite hard to spend money
    during the long vacation. Even though students will need
    new material for the beginning of the next academic year,
    their lecturers often don't think of this until just before the
    year starts, and they forget that it takes time to acquire, pay
    for, catalogue, and prepare the new material for shelving.

9 Writing a business plan

Preparing business plans is part of the work of many senior academic librarians, and it is as well to have an understanding of the principal components of them even if it doesn't form part of your everyday life. The following tips are designed to familiarize you with the elements that often make up a business plan.

1. **Don't do it alone.** Business plans are rarely best done by a single individual, although one person will need to take ultimate responsibility for the final version. Ask everyone who is involved to participate, even if this only means commenting on a draft if time is short. This way the people who it affects most will have a commitment to it.

2. **Begin with a SWOT analysis.** Individually or with colleagues, work out what are the strengths, weaknesses, opportunities and threats facing your area of operation. Use these to get an overall picture of where you are starting from.

3. **Start with your strengths.** These strengths could include your financial status, the team of people you work with, your physical environment, a favourable internal political environment. Look at how can you build upon them and seek ways to exploit them to their full potential.

4. **Work with your weaknesses.** Look where the gaps lie, where your service is not as good as you would hope it to be. Identify what is getting in the way of your operations.

5. **Open up your opportunities.** Ask yourself you can overcome your difficulties, branch out into new areas, identify new areas of activity or take advantage of any new programmes or opportunities that might present themselves. Who can best help you to achieve your aims?

6. **Think about your threats.** What factors will prevent you from achieving what you want to achieve, and how might you be prevented from achieving your targets. What hazards are lurking that might threaten your work? Who or what are your enemies or competitors?

7. **Go on to do a STEP analysis.** Look at the sociological, technological, economic and political factors that impinge upon your work. Ask yourself how these will affect your plans for the future and then use the insights to enrich your plan.

8. **Work out who your customers are.** Obviously, these are primarily your students, but your client group will also include academic and other staff, external users and others. Try to decide what are their various needs are and how these might conflict and coincide.

9. **Clarify your current financial status.** Think clearly about what you have in the way of assets, where your income comes from, what are your liabilities, what are your outgoings. Look at what is fixed, what is likely to get worse and what you can improve upon.

10. **Look for new opportunities.** On your own or (better) with colleagues, brainstorm new developments. Allow this exercise to be creative by not censoring what may seem like daft suggestions: suspend judgement until you have come up with plenty of ideas. Build on existing ideas and allow your thought to run freely.

11. **Play with a nightmare.** Fantasize what things would be like if everything went horribly wrong. Come up with worst case scenarios, identify potential disasters. Use this task to help you clarify what is really important to you and your team and make up a checklist for your planning.

12. **Switch over to a dream.** Visualize what your proposals would be like if everything went swimmingly.. What would be your ideal scenario? Then use this data to help you crystallize your goals and targets.

13. **Investigate the competition.** Who is likely to be competing for your users, especially when you are offering new services? Ask yourself why people would come to you or buy your services, rather than anyone else's.

14. **Base your business plan on data.** Marshall your facts in support of your arguments. As far as possible, support your assertions with numbers, names and data rather than optimistic guesses.

15. **Consider how you would market your services.** How will you reach your internal and external users? Will you use posters, newsletters, e-mail, direct mailing to people you want to target, or other means?

16. **Cost your activities realistically.** If you want to promote your services, what are the real costs involved? Are any of these costs recoverable? Have you taken into account all of the institutional overheads?

17. **Plan for the future.** In the current business plan, look forward to the next stage of development, and suggest what directions you might take in the future.

18. **Plan for contingencies.** Try to make allowances in case things don't work out quite as well as you had hoped. Look at your nightmare scenario, and incorporate the learning from this into your contingency planning exercise.

19. **Draft the plan.** Take time to make sure it looks good, and that the figures add up, and that it reads fluently. Make sure all of the information fits together appropriately. Be rigorous

about eliminating unnecessary detail, and make sure it is concise and to the point.

20. **Get some feedback.** Before you go public with a business plan, show it to colleagues and trusted peers so you can get an outside view before you pass it on to its intended recipients.

10 Managing library environments

Librarians are managers of space and are to a greater or lesser extent responsible for their working environment. Even today relatively few work in purpose-built libraries that could be described as remotely ideal. The fact is that librarians mostly have to make the best out of what they have got with buildings, equipment and furniture. So these tips are aimed towards tweaking the system to try to get the best out of what you've got.

1. **Get to know your cleaning staff.** Things are so much smoother and easier if you are on good working terms with your cleaning staff. Talk to them – try to make them feel a part of the team and appreciated. They are people too.

2. **Plan a system that looks after itself where possible.** For example, if you don't want food or drinks causing mess in the library, appropriate rules about what can be taken in are one step. Another step, however, is to contain such problems in a separate area which is relatively easy to keep well cleaned. You may argue that few librarians are themselves involved in policy decisions of these kinds, but they are the ideal people to inform the policy decision-makers.

3. **Get to know your caretakers or servicing staff.** This is very important. They are often a mine of information about the site. Not only do they know vital information about the life-functions of your building, they probably know more about the internal politics of the institution than you do and will be the first to hear of any significant news. If you need to get something done quickly they will know where to start and can often pull strings. If you get on the right side of them

it can make your life much easier – if you get on the wrong side it can be very difficult.

4. **Know where all the fuses are!** First, though, get good health and safety training, so that you are authorized as well as competent to attend to minor electrical problems. Make sure that each fuse is clearly labelled with which power supplies it controls. This can save accidentally turning all sorts of equipment off when looking for which circuit has a problem. If a relay keeps cutting out, the most likely cause is that there's too much on a particular circuit.

5. **Learn the procedure for getting minor works done.** There will be some sort of system for this. Again find out who the electricians or carpenters are: it can make a lot of difference if you need to get some repairs done quickly.

6. **Have your own desk-collection of tools!** Over the years you will be amazed how many times you use screwdrivers to extricate a CD or computer disk from its drive, a hammer to persuade home a piece of bent shelving, a bradawl to help put screws into walls. It is also very useful to know where you can get access to a long ladder and trolleys. Other essentials include oil for doors which squeak.

7. **Try to get some control of your heating and ventilation.** This may or may not be possible depending on your situation, and the security arrangements on your campus. But it is highly desirable to be able to turn the heating up or down or to be able to open or close windows if you so wish. It is remarkable how few librarians are in a position to do even this. If you have no control then at least make sure you have fans for summer and electric fires for winter.

8. **Build mess patrols into routine procedures.** Libraries have the propensity to become untidy very quickly unless active measures are taken. Piles of books or journals, pieces

of shelving, cardboard boxes and so on tend to get dumped somewhere and just left unless someone comes along and asks what they are doing there. So at regular intervals patrol for mess and try to instil this as a habit into all staff. Avoid it being 'someone else's problem' which is what can happen if everyone only controls the mess in their own area.

9. **Get at least some natural light.** If it is at all possible try to organize your workspace so that you get some natural daylight. This should in fact be covered by the health and safety procedures for your institution. If this is not possible and you have to work under strip lighting for extended periods, keep some spare tubes to replace ones which start to flicker.

10. **Be on the look out for the early signs of infestation.** Libraries contain a lot of organic matter, not least books and carpets. For obvious reasons it is best to catch any infestations early. Watch out particularly around kitchens or vending machines if you have them. Don't forget the lesser life forms: carpets can catch fleas, and even books can become infested. Even computers can catch viruses!

11. **Think green!** It can make a significant difference to a library to have at least some green plants around the place. There needs to be someone with the responsibility to water them and look after them properly.

12. **Be on the lookout for potential hazards.** Health and safety legislation obliges librarians to do this anyway, but safety is best regarded as a good habit and not an obligatory duty. Look out for trailing wires, fire exits which are obstructed, and any shelving which is unstable.

13. **Label your keys.** Ideally, all keys should be in key boxes, and be correctly ordered and labelled. There are few things worse than not being able to find the key to the 3rd alarmed door on the 4th floor corridor, when the alarm is ringing!

14. **Regularly clean machinery.** Computer terminals can get disgustingly grubby very quickly in busy libraries, as can the glass plates of photocopiers. Even minor things like hole punches and staplers need someone to clean them, and empty them or fill them. Cleaning staff can not be expected to look after all these details, and may be afraid to clean (for example) computer keyboards in case something irretrievable may happen with the computer.

15. **Audit your artistic talents!** It can be useful to identify a member of staff who has a flair for arranging poster displays or exhibitions, and helping such a person to add some visual interest to suitable parts of the library from time to time.

16. **Keep notices to a minimum.** Notice-boards can quickly become very cluttered, as students (and others) put out publicity materials for all sorts of things. Few people actually *read* notice boards, and even fewer if they are cluttered. Sticking notices up on walls with Blu-Tack is also to be avoided, as they can rarely be removed without some damage or mess.

11 Managing noise

There are no easy solutions to the problem of noise. It is rather like a garden: if you can keep it under some control then you are doing well. However, when people talk to each other, they learn a lot that they could not learn just from looking at books or computer screens. The following suggestions may help both towards a quieter life and towards an effective learning environment for users.

1. **Accept that students have views about noise.** The attitude of a lot of students is 'I want to work in quiet conditions *and* to be able to make a lot of noise when I want to'. Very few students are prepared to ask others to be quiet. Those students who actually complain about noise often have loud voices themselves and are oblivious of the fact. There is almost a collective denial of responsibility – it is seen by many students as the librarians' problem and they may treat you as though you must solve it.

2. **It is not only a student problem!** Groups of mature students are often no better and academic staff – despite the insistence of some of them policy-making committees that total, sepulchral silence must reign at all times – are almost the worst offenders of all. The decibel prize, however, often goes to caretakers and delivery men to whom silence is an alien concept.

3. **Recognize that some noise is legitimate.** Students are asked to work in groups and therefore have to talk in a group and work with library resources at the same time. Librarians in many institutions have encouraged and supported group learning, so they have to allocate physical space to it. This needs to be appropriate open space, with open tables, and

separated by doors from areas where silence is still thought to be golden.

4. **Lead by example.** If you have to talk to anyone in an area that has been deemed to be a silent area, don't! Or at least whisper as you lead the person to somewhere where it is acceptable to talk. If library staff don't follow their own rules, they can't expect users to either.

5. **Zone your study space into quiet and group study areas.** Then if a group is making a noise you can provide them with an alternative and ask: 'Would you mind moving to the other area please?' This is a quiet study area'. This can be done politely without putting students backs up. It is useful if the zoning can be done so that people proceeding to the quiet area go through a door or barrier marked 'quiet area beyond this point'.

6. **Recognize that traffic is noisy.** It is naturally more difficult to maintain low levels of noise in parts of the building where people are coming and going frequently. Also, enquiry points and help-points are likely to make their own noise, so it is best to accept that the areas where users and library staff are expected to talk should not be regarded as quiet areas.

7. **Allow students to book in advance 'noisy areas'.** For example, if your building has the luxury of small tutorial or seminar rooms, sealed off from the main study areas, students planning to do some collaborative work will be only too pleased to reserve such a location in advance. Issuing keys at the main desk can be a problem, though, as you won't always get the keys back! Therefore, it is better that such areas are not kept locked, or are unlocked by library staff on request.

8. **Physically divide your work spaces.** This will put up barriers against noise but the space becomes less flexible in terms of potential usage. Open plan space is more flexible

but noise becomes more intrusive. Physical dividers can at least place some limits on how many students find it workable to talk to one another at a time. Physical dividers into single study spaces encourage individual work, while tables which seat two or four, without dividers, encourage pair-work or small-group work.

9. **Consider putting study desks or tables in among the less-popular stacks.** Little quiet 'study islands' can be formed, where it is only really possible for one person to sit working there, and the only distraction should be people visiting the stacks. Those students who really want to find a quiet private place quickly discover such 'islands'.

10. **Establish and label a 'silence' area.** If there is a particular area where silence is going to prevail, those students who really wish to study quietly will head for it. It needs to be an area where there is as little as possible noise from other sources too, for example from outside the building. This eases the tension in other parts of the library where noise is allowed (if not encouraged).

11. **Identify the areas that are most likely to be noisy.** This may influence your choice of furniture for these areas. You may want to put in study carrels, so that students can work in quiet conditions amid the hustle and bustle outside.

12. **Put up appropriate notices.** Librarians have to have notices up because if they don't the first thing their users will say is 'you have a noise problem – so put notices up'. Just don't expect anybody to take any notice of notices. The problem with them is that they very quickly become part of the background, which people don't see any more. To counter this effect, try to ensure that notices have status and are strategically placed. A good location for such notices is actually *on* study desks in areas intended to be quiet ones. It is

useful to put notices about quiet and less-quiet areas where people will see them as they enter and leave the library.

13. **Ask people politely to be quiet.** This may work for some groups of students: mature students, for example. For most 18–21 year olds however it is more likely to be ignored. The noise level dips and then after a few minutes goes back to its original level.

14. **Ask insistently for people to be quiet.** This will work for some groups of students but for other groups there can be problems. Some students tend to single out those members of the library staff who insist on silence, and a climate of resentment can develop. If asking for cooperation is not working, it is time to try alternative combinations of strategies from this list.

15. **Minimize direct confrontations.** If there are frequent confrontations, a certain bloody-mindedness may set in. Librarians may lose the cooperation of users and the place is no quieter than before. Also, it takes an enormous physical and mental toll on you, the librarian.

16. **Don't reduce noise just to please the academic staff.** Some expect librarians to be authority figures and are happier when they are. It shows that you are taking the problem of noise seriously and are trying to do something about it. So they may approve of the big stick – as long as it is not applied to them.

17. **Be clear in your own mind what is acceptable.** Agree with colleagues what is an acceptable noise level for each area, and what is acceptable noise-reducing behaviour and what is not. This needs to be discussed with all staff and should be reflected in the library rules. It is worth admitting that librarians, computer staff and technical staff are likely to

have different feelings about what an acceptable level of noise might be.

18. **Accept that it is impossible to be absolutely fair.** After all, librarians do not possess a 'noiseometer'. They will tend to pick on groups that work in their vicinity, or they may come down on a relatively minor misdemeanour after allowing a number of other greater ones to go unchecked.

19. **Try to encourage user responsibility.** See if there are ways of building noise regulation in the library into the student charter, so that students themselves have some ownership of the rules.

20. **Start each year as you would like to continue.** Try to make your position clear on noise early in the academic year. If librarians get into the habit of having a quiet library it may well continue. Once the noise habit sets in it can be very difficult to break.

Chapter 3
Supporting students

Much of the work of academic librarians relates in one way or another to the business of supporting students in their learning on the courses in our institutions. Many other parts of this book overlap with the particular aspects which we have grouped into this chapter.

We begin this chapter with suggestions on helping students to learn about the library. It is not surprising that we ended up with more than 30 suggestions on aspects of this topic.

We next move to another principal area of the work of many people in libraries, that of dealing with enquiries. This too led us to quite an extended set of suggestions, but we would emphasize that you may need to be selective regarding the implementation these: there is not time in the average librarian's life to allow every one of these to be put into practice.

Next, we turn our attention to international students. Such students make up differing proportions of the population of different institutions, but their needs can be sufficiently distinctive to warrant us thinking separately about them, while remembering that libraries need to provide a service to the whole student community without showing favour or discrimination of any kind.

Another group of students who share distinctive characteristics are part-time students, and in many institutions the proportion of part-time students continues to grow quite rapidly. Essentially, with part-time students librarians are dealing with mature people, who know their own minds, and whose time is much more limited than that of their counterparts on full-time courses. We hope our suggestions will help you to treat them accordingly.

A further group of students who may need additional, targeted support is those with special needs. Such students can include those with specific problem areas including hearing, seeing, learning, and mobility. We offer some suggestions about how library staff can do their part to ensure that students with these needs can make the most of their learning opportunities in libraries.

We end this chapter with some suggestions on helping students to use the Internet productively. Increasingly, students make their learning strides with the new technologies in environments such as libraries rather than in classrooms, so librarians have an important (and interesting) role to play. As with our section on computers in Chapter 1, we are aware that many colleagues in academic libraries will have skills in the use of the Internet which make our own attempts pale into insignificance. Our suggestions under this heading are intended for people who are starting off on this pathway, and should be skipped by all our colleagues with considerable expertise.

12 Helping students to learn about the library

Helping students to learn about the library is a never-ending process. The goal is to empower students to be able to use the resources of the library for themselves – but librarians know how few students actually manage to do this. Still it is important to keep on trying. User induction takes many forms, from general tours, or the special sessions for students about to undertake a major piece of work, to the day-to-day processes of one-to-one support and help. The following suggestions should help your students to make good use of the library.

1. **Be enthusiastic when doing user education!** When groups of students are timetabled to come in to learn about the library, it is a fair assumption to expect them to regard it as a fairly boring process. A bit of enthusiasm and fun can go a long way to convince students that the library is an attractive and valuable resource for them.

2. **Don't assume anything!** You can't afford to assume that new students will come to your college all set to make the most of any library they encounter. Sadly, nor can you assume that final year degree students will have gone all the way up the learning curve of using the library – some may hardly have been through your doors! So, one of the tasks for the staff of any college library is to help students, new and old, to get started on making the most of what's on offer. Here are some tips to start off with.

3. **Don't assume that academic staff will help students to learn about the library.** Some will, and will do it very well. However, there is no lack of academic staff who themselves

have not developed the sorts of skills we wish students to develop.

4. **Find out where you need to start.** Get yourself armed with some gentle questions you can pose to students, to find out whether they need your help in starting from scratch, or whether they're already quite familiar with how the library works.

5. **Get the outside view.** When librarians work in a library every day, they become so familiar with it that it is easy for them not to be able to see the sorts of problems that new users could find. It can be useful to get someone from outside to cast a fresh eye over the way that the library works, and to comment on how easy they find it to make sense of the guides, instructions, equipment, and the staff.

6. **Have a variety of ways that students can learn.** Some students will learn all they need to get started from an official 'tour' at induction. Others will prefer a self-study booklet allowing them to find their own way round things. Some will prefer to explore alone, others in groups. Some will like to ask, others will want to do it all without direct help. Some will like to sit at a keyboard and find out all they need from a computer. Accommodate as many approaches as possible.

7. **Make learning about the library fun!** Here, we're thinking particularly about training sessions and induction tours. Don't assume that because you think libraries are the most fascinating places on earth that students will share your view. Tickle their imaginations; for example if you set a task for students involving finding something in the library, make it something that will make them smile when they find it.

8. **Legitimize appropriate group working.** Tell students that it is indeed OK for them to work in groups, for example when using self-instructional workbooks or worksheets. Students

learn a lot from each other, and can do so in the library, provided such work is done in the right areas of the library.

9. **Consider assessing library induction.** Some courses make the library orientation activity an assessed task, so that students are motivated to undertake it. Showing that librarians place a high value on the skills and knowledge that students acquire may make some of them more committed to the task.

10. **Link library activities with other assignments that students are doing.** For example, a librarian can be part of a team assessing students' work, perhaps helping to assess a content-based piece of work on aspects to do with information retrieval and selection, alongside academics assessing the subject-based parts. This sort of assignment is more useful and memorable to students than something they perceive just as a 'library assignment, one-off and forgettable'.

11. **Make it easy for them to remember what you tell them.** Give them aide-mémoires such as bookmarks with the relevant shelf numbers for their subject area, pens with the university opening hours on or big colourful graphics on the walls to reinforce their learning about the library.

12. **Introduce them gently.** Remember that students may never have used a large library before and may be totally unfamiliar with catalogues, shelf numbering systems and information retrieval systems. Some may also be daunted and terrified by the sheer size of the place and may feel very anxious and out of their depth. We are not trying to turn students into librarians, so stay away from the jargon of librarianship as far as is possible.

13. **Let them know the rules of the game.** Let them know where they can talk, eat and drink, smoke and do group work, so they know what to expect. Make it clear how much help

they can reasonably expect, and what kinds of tasks they should be doing for themselves.

14. **Give them a map.** Students may need help to understand the organization or the layout of the library, so give them something visual to help them.

15. **Be prepared for high IT demands.** Students coming from well-equipped school libraries or from abroad may be used to much higher levels of IT than your library can support, so don't be surprised if they demand more than you can offer.

16. **It's not just about books.** Some students may be used to very conventional libraries, with few facilities other than texts. Make students aware of the range of resources libraries have to offer and the ways in which these can support their studies.

17. **Get students doing things themselves.** For example, it's not much good just showing students how to use computer-ized catalogues. Ask them to input some data themselves, and watch what they do. Often, any mistakes they make are very simple, such as putting in an unnecessary initial in front of an author's name, or getting into the wrong menu.

18. **Don't forget to smile!** Induction is a bewildering process for new students. If librarians do induction tours then probably the most valuable thing they can do is to walk them around the space and smile at them. They will forget your name but may not forget your face, and if they feel that librarians are approachable you have already achieved something useful.

19. **Make induction relevant.** Don't tell them all about abstracts and indexes before they need to use them. Work closely with tutors, so that you can drip-feed information to students as they need it or want it.

20. **Show things rather than talk about them.** Students will retain practically nothing of what you say. Librarians have to try to make the tour as 'physical' as possible: 'this is a library card', 'this is the issue desk', 'this is a weekly loan book' and 'this is a short loan book'.

21. **Keep induction short.** Choose a few key pieces of information that you wish to put across and don't try to do any more than that. There is no point in talking for more than 10 minutes or as long as it takes to walk them around the library. As soon as you see the eyes beginning to glaze over – stop!

22. **Sit them down for really important things.** A lot of librarians try to talk as they are walking – this usually means that most of the students in the group don't hear. For the essential information, make sure the group is sitting down somewhere comfortable and they can all hear what you say. The group will often appreciate a rest but don't make it long enough to be boring.

23. **Avoid reading from a prepared script.** Few people like being read to, after they've advanced beyond bedtime stories. A read-out script rarely sounds as sincere or as secure as a fresh address. By all means use notes, prompts, keywords and checklists to remind you what you're going to say, but avoid the temptation to write it all out, except for the purposes of putting it into print in a handout or a guide.

24. **Use handouts for induction.** The most important information that you have told people should be duplicated in a handout and given out to all students at the end of the session. It is best if this is a sheet of A4 so that it can go into a student folder. There may be little point in giving them a library guide book which will probably contain too much information and so will not be read. It may be better for students to take the responsibility of getting their own copies of such guides

when they choose to do this, and then they will value them more than if they're simply given them.

25. **Plan the timing of induction.** Ideally, induction works best when students actually *need* it. For example, it can be useful to tie induction into the first piece of assessed work if this is at all possible. Students will only really start to learn about the library when they need to use it to do their coursework.

26. **Don't make induction 'unmissable'!** For all sorts of reasons, there will be students who don't make it to their allotted induction tour. They may enrol on their courses late, or may be otherwise engaged at the time, or may not bother to turn up. It is important that they can make up in other ways for what they missed.

27. **Some people don't like being inducted.** Accommodate people who would rather learn about the library in their own ways. Library guides, and one-topic handouts can be viable alternatives to induction tours.

28. **Remember that some students will already know a lot.** Some students may have had extensive experience in other good libraries, while for others much will be new. Try to keep in mind that you will be dealing with mixed-experience groups of students, and avoid patronizing those who already know things.

29. **Use students' *shared* experience.** When illustrating points, especially for first-year students, use examples from popular culture rather than assuming academic knowledge.

30. **Consider having advertised 'open to all' induction tours.** These can be available at various times of the year, and at different times of the day and week. See what the demand is, for example by having 'signing-up' sheets, and running as

many such tours as are popular. At least you know that you'll be doing induction for students who *want* to be inducted.

31. **Keep students informed about new services.** When introducing a new service or facility, plan several ways of getting the word around about it, including short, easy-to-read fliers, demonstrations, posters and circulars to departments.

13   Dealing with enquiries

Librarians spend much of their time and energy dealing with questions from students. For the person asking the question, it may seem like the most important question in the world at the time. Students often seem to need some help to ensure that they ask the right questions in the first place. The librarian may have answered the same question 20 times already that day so clearly, this is an area where librarians need to develop patience, and efficiency. Many of the suggestions below are also relevant to enquiries from academic staff and other users, but since most enquiries tend to come from students we've placed them in this chapter.

1. **Be seen immediately as wanting to help.** In practice, as we'll explain in several of the suggestions below, librarians will often have to do a fair amount of asking and clarifying before they are in a position to get down to doing some real helping. However, it is important that enquirers don't feel that they are being subjected to interrogation.

2. **People almost never ask for what they actually want.** For example, 'I want a map of Surrey' could turn out to be a request for the address of a hotel which is not in fact in Surrey but Hampshire. A common complaint amongst enquiry desk staff is that after they have spent half an hour tracking down something they find they have been barking up the wrong tree. So even if someone asks for something directly, it can be helpful to find out more about why they need it.

3. **People sometimes don't know what they want.** People don't always come into the library with well thought out ideas on how they are going to approach an essay question or

what information they need to gather for a project. They sometimes start with the vaguest notions. Librarians may usefully help them to define the ideas that are floating around in their minds via a question and answer process.

4. **Gather as much information as you can.** Depending on the circumstances, any or all of the following questions may help librarians to deal with the enquiry: 'Are you a student here?', 'Which course are you on?', 'What piece of work are you doing?', 'Which lecturer has told you to do this?', 'What exactly have you been told to do?'. Such questions provide useful pointers to the level of information that the students require.

5. **Try to see the lecturer's instructions to the students.** When students have printed briefings, they often don't read them very carefully, or even misinterpret them in the same ways that they often misinterpret exam questions. It can be very helpful for the students if librarians take them through the instructions, helping them to see exactly what they are intended to do. Sometimes, however, the fault will be with the instructions, which may be confusing, or even asking students to do the impossible, and librarians may have to advise students to seek further clarification from the lecturer involved.

6. **'Is it 500 words you've been told to write, or 5000?'** First year students may just want the most basic information on a topic, whereas final year students may be doing an entire project on the same topic.

7. **'Is it an essay you're going to do, or a presentation, or a group project?'** Finding out in which format students are going to present their work is a useful indicator of the sorts of materials that will be most suitable for them to investigate.

8. **Try to understand the subject area yourself.** There is no way you can ever develop enough subject knowledge to be able to answer all possible enquiries. Instead, you have to become adept at asking questions, and homing in on exactly what is wanted. Always ask the enquirer to explain to you any terms that you don't understand. If they ask something highly specific, try to identify it within a broader subject area.

9. **Don't forget current affairs.** Students are often set tasks arising from something topical that may have been mentioned by their lecturers, and they are usually asked to include some discussion of current trends in work that they are writing. It is very helpful in dealing with their enquiries to know what has been in the news recently.

10. **Keep yourself abreast of the stock that is most relevant to frequent enquiries.** You may find it particularly worthwhile to look for new information as it arises in sources such as directories and yearbooks, as well as in journals and websites. It is always a good feeling when you are able to reply to an enquirer: 'Oh yes, I know exactly where you can find that'.

11. **Think of yourself as a detective.** If you have a difficult enquiry and are not sure where to go to solve it, start by assuming that the answer is in the library. It often is, and you may just have to look long enough and hard enough for it. Another possibility is to ask colleagues who know the answer already. Very few people will think any the less of you because you can't solve a particular enquiry straight away. What they appreciate is your time, your attention and the effort you are making on their behalf.

12. **Don't worry if you can't solve a particular enquiry straight away.** Very few people will think the less of you if you have to say 'I'll try to find out more about this by tomor-

row at the same time' or 'I'll need to ask around my colleagues and find out who knows most about this'. What people do appreciate is your time, your attention, and the efforts you are making on their behalf.

13. **Sometimes, enquiries need to be referred on.** For example, the most appropriate agency to deal with some enquiries may be the students' own departmental office, another library, a professional body or organization, and so on.

14. **Don't pass enquirers on unnecessarily.** There is little worse when enquiring than being passed around from person to person, and having to repeat exactly what you're looking for. Therefore, refer enquirers on only when they will get better help from someone else, and not because you're too busy to deal with them.

15. **Acknowledge people who are waiting.** The nature of enquiry work is that some enquiries can be dealt with in seconds whereas others can take up to half an hour or longer. It is important to acknowledge the presence of people who may be waiting and to tell them you will be with them as soon as possible. Sometimes, you may be wise to ask the person who needs a longer spell of your time to give you a few minutes to deal first with some routine matters for other people waiting.

16. **Encourage questions.** Librarians have to recognize that people often feel stupid about asking questions and often hover, uncertain whether or not to ask. If you are staffing an enquiry point, realize that being there to answer questions is your priority so don't hide behind some other task. Be on the lookout for those who might be plucking up courage to ask, and make contact with them rather than waiting for them to make the initiative.

17. **Agree how long the student has before the answer is needed.** When the answer is not needed immediately, you can (for example) arrange to send a printout or document through the internal mail within an agreed time, or reply using e-mail. You can if necessary arrange a further appointment.

18. **Do your best for people.** People often come to the library for information because they have been fobbed off somewhere else. There is nothing worse than a librarian giving someone the cold shoulder, because they would rather be doing something else or can't be bothered. Librarians are sometimes seen as the last resort if all else fails, or the most likely people to take any enquiry seriously.

19. **Don't point, take.** Telling a student that what they want is in the 650s, that the journals are shelved in alphabetical order or pointing 'over there' may not be a lot of use. Students do find libraries confusing and the guiding systems may not be a lot of help. Where possible take them and show them: it is a nice touch and is usually appreciated.

20. **Never trust a book list.** Never assume that any information on a book list is accurate. Always check it. Also don't assume that students have got information correctly from the catalogue – in the long run you save a lot of time by always checking.

21. **Keep enquiry cards.** These are records of all the more-difficult or more-important enquiries librarians have answered. Librarians may need little more than a keyword or two for filing the question asked and the outcome. In time this builds up into a useful data bank of information about requests, and can be used for staff training exercises.

14 Supporting international students

Academic libraries are often used by students who speak many languages. Quite frequently, English is not their strongest one. Student users come from all kinds of cultures and backgrounds, both from within the UK and from abroad and they may find local conditions different and confusing. Sometimes they are homesick, alienated and unsure of the new circumstances in which they find themselves. All students need to be treated in the same way, and in order to have an equivalent study experience everyone needs to learn to fit into the same systems and procedures. However, some international students will need some extra help and support to reach such a position. The following suggestions may alert librarians to some of the main issues to bear in mind.

1. **Help gently with acculturation issues.** International students can seem very different in their demands and expectations. Some will be really grateful for any thing librarians do to help them, while others will seem to take a great deal for granted. Some students may come from relatively privileged circumstances, and be used to other people doing the running around for them. In these cases, it can take some time for them to attune to the levels of self-reliance expected of them. It is important that in the library and elsewhere, we make clear what are the groundrules for all concerned.

2. **Beware of making assumptions.** Don't assume that students have or have not been born in Britain simply by their appearance. Test out assumptions of language fluency and try to ensure that you pitch your advice and support at the level of the user, rather than according to your preconceptions of

what they may or may not understand. Avoid patronizing, over-simplifying or just speaking very loudly, but pause at intervals to check understanding when you feel students are struggling to keep up with you.

3. **Whenever possible, write things down for students who may not be following your directions.** International students can otherwise end up spending ages searching for something they have written down incorrectly, have spelled wrongly or have misheard. Librarians can usually tell by students' body language whether they have really understood what they have said, but it is often worth checking by paraphrasing or asking them a few questions. Similarly, when you can't understand what they are saying to you, ask them to write it down for you. Take, rather than point. For students who have difficulty with spoken instructions, it can be quite daunting to have to try to remember a series of directions. It is often quicker (and more welcoming) to accompany such students to the places they need to find, at least on the first occasion they ask for assistance.

4. **Don't interpret lack of English language skills as an indicator of lack of ability.** Speak clearly, avoiding jargon, colloquialisms and masses of acronyms and look at your hearer. Reinforce what you are saying by showing how to use equipment, by diagrams or by notes. Similarly, when international students don't seem willing to answer your questions, don't interpret it as rudeness. They may still be working out what your questions actually mean. In sessions when you are speaking to a whole group and there is a background murmur of noise, be aware that they may be translating for one another.

5. **Think about providing user-guides is different languages.** When your institution attracts significant contingents from different cultures, it may be worth having key

support materials translated into the appropriate languages. Alternatively, special help-sheets in different languages can be designed to help such groups of students to address particular problems.

6. **Keep your distance!** People from some cultures find body contact offensive or threatening, so be careful to respect their personal space when demonstrating equipment, online systems and so on. In some cultures, making eye contact is considered disrespectful, whereas in others, failure to do so leads to accusations of shiftiness. The frequency of smiling and the use of 'please' and 'thank you' varies also.

7. **Don't assume that international students will understand the classification systems you use.** Systems vary considerably world-wide, and though students may be well up on how to use the system they were familiar with, they may need extra support to learn a new system.

8. **Be aware that international students can have very different experiences of technology in libraries.** Some may have expectations of superb information technology facilities, and be sorely disappointed by your provision, while others may find the technology you have available hopelessly daunting. Both of these groups of students need sensitive and understanding support.

9. **Be ready to clarify issues that may be different in your institution's learning environment.** For example, in some cultures, respect for teachers may mean that they consider it impertinent to try to improve on the tutor's words by rephrasing them and this can lead to accusations of plagiarism. Similarly, the borderlines between what is called collaboration and cheating can be interpreted differently, especially where strongly bonded groups of students are very committed to supporting one another. International students some-

times need sensitive counselling and explanations to help them to tune in to the new expectations they may meet on such issues.

10. **Be prepared to act on occasions more like a tutor than a librarian.** International students who are part of large classes may have very limited opportunities to ask academic staff for guidance or help, and the fact that it is easier for them to talk to you may result in them bringing you the problems that would usually be dealt with by their academic tutor. It is possible you will feel able to deal with some of this work yourself, but you may find it more appropriate to refer students on to the relevant academic colleague, or perhaps to seek the help of fellow students, who will often be well placed to assist.

15   Supporting part-time students

Part-time students make up an increasing proportion of the users of academic libraries. While in most respects, all students need to be treated equally in the design of library systems and processes, it remains possible to go that extra step to help part-timers with their particular needs.

1.   **Remember that part-time students don't have much time.** They are often combining a busy career with study and family responsibilities. They therefore will often appreciate a little bit of extra help, for example when it comes to finding things in the library.

2.   **Part-time students may miss out on induction.** They may well not be enrolled at the same time that full-time students are being inducted, and indeed part-time enrolments tend to be more flexible anyway. It is useful to have an ongoing programme of induction opportunities that part-timers can reserve places on, or to make alternative induction formats available to them, such as videos, guidance booklets, or 'how to' sheets.

3.   **Part-time students often need places for group work.** The library may be the only suitable place open to them in the evenings, and the times when they can participate in group work may be quite specific and limited. Encouraging them to make full use of any facilities and to book rooms in advance can help to solve this problem for them.

4.   **Part-time students have different study-skills needs.** They may indeed be expert in time-management and task-management skills, but not aware of their own expertise in such areas, with resulting general lack of confidence about

their approaches to study. It can be valuable to offer them suggestions about the most useful study-skills resource materials specifically directed towards part-time students.

5. **Part-time students often can't come back tomorrow.** This means that the sorts of occasion on which you may suggest to full-time students that you will sort something out for them by the next day need to be handled differently for part-timers.

6. **It can be worth having some set texts specifically reserved for part-time students.** When the same resources are in demand from both full-time and part-time students, it may be quite impossible for part-timers to arrive early enough to get the best chance of acquiring these. A separate collection of well-chosen key resources will be put to effective use by part-time students.

7. **Encourage part-time students to make good use of online support and information services.** For many of them it is relatively easy for them to log-on to such services from their own workplaces, and they may be able to make their visits to the library much more productive by working out in advance what they want to look at, and whom they may wish to talk to.

8. **Part-timers are likely to visit the library less frequently.** It is therefore understandable that they may forget how to use systems, and how equipment works. Even when you remember explaining something to some given part-time students some time ago, a lot may have happened in their lives since then, and it is necessary to be patient enough to explain things once more when necessary.

9. **Part-time students may be nervous about using a large library.** Particularly when using the library for the first time, it can seem daunting to them. Mature students are often

unwilling to admit that they need help, and it can be useful to watch out for signs of them experiencing difficulties.

10. **Some part-time students have a 'supermarket dash' approach in the library.** They can be desperate to clear the shelves of everything that could turn out to be relevant to them, simply because they don't have the time to study the available stock and select wisely. When possible, help them with advice about the stock that most students find useful.

16 Supporting students with special needs

Colleges have a responsibility to provide the best possible educational opportunities within their remit for all students. Open-access policies, together with statutory requirements, mean that librarians need to take into account the requirements of students with special needs when planning library provision. These suggestions are designed to help you think about how best to approach this.

1. **Adopt a positive action approach.** Students with special needs should not be regarded as a problem to be dealt with, rather as a constituency of users whose needs must be taken into account. The importance of consdiering students with special needs in an 'inclusive' way has recently been emphasized in the UK in the FEFC Report (1996) on 'Inclusive Learning' (see Further Reading for details).

2. **Involve the students in managing the support you offer.** The people who are most affected are usually the best to advise you on appropriate support strategies. They should be consulted alongside specialist external advisers when designing your provision.

3. **Think carefully about the language you use.** For example, the term 'handicapped' can cause offence, since it is derived from those who came 'cap in hand' to ask for help. 'Disability' can also be seen as a derogatory term, suggesting something of less value than ability. People with special needs usually prefer to be regarded as people first and last, rather than being categorized by what they can't do.

4. **Don't assume that people with mobility problems are wheelchair-bound.** Most people entitled to use the UK orange badge on their vehicles are not, in fact, users of wheelchairs. They may, however, experience difficulties in walking long distances, climbing stairs, or undertaking other strenuous activities. Be aware of whose special needs may not be at all apparent, such as people with asthma and heart problems.

5. **Don't use difficult buildings as an excuse to exclude people with special needs.** It can be expensive and difficult to install lifts, automatic doors and ramps, especially into old buildings, but lateral thinking can work miracles. It may be impossible to arrange that people with special needs have access to the whole of your building, but it is usually possible to ensure that help can be made available to them from a point that they can reach without difficulty. It is important that such help is provided promptly, without them becoming embarrassed by waiting.

6. **Help people with visual impairments.** Colleges can do much to help students who don't see well to study effectively. For example, allowing students to tape-record classes, and making available on loan recording equipment from the college can help considerably. Visual impairment is frequently not total, and librarians can help by using large font sizes on overhead transparencies in any library induction programmes attended by such users. The mobility of people with visual impairments can be improved moderately easily by such means as Braille signing, tactile strips on corridor floors, and 'talking' lifts.

7. **Help students with hearing difficulties.** Many colleges now have audio loop systems which enable students to amplify sound in classrooms, and it can be useful if librarians are aware of which rooms are so equipped. Similar systems at

important contact points in the library can be very helpful. These can be supplemented by individual librarians speaking particularly clearly when working with such users.

8. **Make provision for students with learning difficulties.** These students cope well in colleges, especially when given additional targeted support as required both in the classroom and around the college and particularly in libraries and learning resource centres. It is important to ensure that students with learning difficulties can fully contribute to the life of the institution. Learning resources centres can be especially helpful in providing a range of resources to support the learning of these students.

9. **Recognize that it is important to provide support for students with, and recovering from, mental illness.** Individual counselling and guidance can be enormously beneficial in enabling these students to use college study as part of a program of personal recovery and development. It is useful if librarians are aware of those students who may need such additional support, and can be as helpful as possible to them.

10. **Keep in mind health and safety requirements for students with special needs.** For example, procedures for fire or bomb-threat evacuation need to take account of those people who cannot move fast, may not hear or see warnings, or who may be unduly alarmed by emergency situations. Ensure that your strategies for coping with emergencies of all kinds take account of the special needs of all of your users.

11. **Seek out additional support.** Check whether there is any source of additional funding to help meet the special needs of users. Funding bodies often have finance available to help institutions meet identified needs of this sort.

17 Helping students to use the Internet productively

Students using the Internet in the library are a client group that is now very significant in most academic libraries. It is useful if most members of library staff are able to help students just starting out on such access to get under way painlessly and efficiently. The following suggestions may help librarians to support students on their first steps in this direction.

1. **Be well informed about what students must do before they can log on.** Make sure you know how they should go about getting their usernames, passwords, and any other registration in your institution before they can access online services or e-mail.

2. **Be willing to talk students through logging on for the first time.** There always has to be a first time, and this will often be at a terminal in the library. It's not much use doing it for students, as they have to learn to do it for themselves, so talking them through the process is the most productive process. It's useful to check whether they've grasped the principles or not, and worth getting them to log off, and then log on again by themselves, with you still close enough to give help again if they have forgotten a step somewhere along the line.

3. **Help students to use the Internet for information retrieval.** Practise using the Internet yourself to locate sources on a topic you are interested in, and find out how to use the various search engines to browse through what is available. You can then show students how you would find

such information as an example of the processes they should practise using themselves.

4. **Demystify the process for technophobes.** Provide easy-to-read user guides, or help people locate guidance materials on the Internet itself. Reinforce to people that they don't have to understand HTML but can use short-cuts to format their own text to make the basis of pages for the Internet.

5. **Introduce students to the various browsers, and show them how to make their own bookmarks.** This makes it easier for students to navigate backwards and forwards, and to focus on the things that prove to be most relevant to their searches.

6. **Emphasize the importance of learning by playing.** Emphasize how useful it is to learn rapidly about the Net just by surfing and exploring quite randomly. Even a few minutes spent doing this can be a valuable learning experience in its own right, and students can pick up many of the principles involved without even realizing how much they are learning at the time.

7. **Encourage students to learn from one another.** There is usually a student at a nearby terminal who has already gone some way up the learning curve with the Internet. Students who have already discovered their own ways of making use of the Web are usually only too keen to share their enthusiasm and experience with others who are just starting out.

8. **Help students to discover the joys and perils of e-mail.** Tell them about any in-house training and guidance that may be available, and help them to get started by talking them through sending you a short message and logging on to a short reply that you send to them straight away.

9. **Provide students with information about relevant discussion lists in their own disciplines.** There are thousands of such lists, so it is worth you exploring the most useful ones from time to time, so you can advise students regarding which lists they may wish to investigate first.

10. **Help students to avoid frustration with the Internet.** For example, tell them where and when the most frustrating log-jams are to be experienced. For example, communications are often much more rapid at times of day when fewer Americans are awake. Also, it can take too long to download complex graphics when the system is at its busiest.

Chapter 4
Supporting academic staff

We devote this chapter to the cause of building up an effective working relationship with the academic staff, who are the most influential group of professional people librarians work alongside. There has not always been a mutually supportive relationship between academic staff and librarians, and this is indeed unfortunate when we think about the complementary roles they play with them in backing-up students' learning.

Our first set of suggestions 'Liaising with academics' tackles some of the fundamental principles which can ensure that librarians work together with them effectively and smoothly. We then move on to 'Working with course committees', which is an area that can be mutually beneficial to academics, their students, and indeed to librarians.

Our next set of suggestions is about working with educational development colleagues. More often than not, they are already converted to the importance of the role that resource-based learning plays in the overall picture of learning in our institutions, and they are among the first to understand the problems that librarians can face in backing-up such learning in libraries. They make good allies, and can help librarians to work towards the goals that they wish to achieve, and we hope that our suggestions will help you to make the most of this convergence of intent.

Supporting academic staff

Next, we turn our attention to the topic of resource-based learning in general terms. Academic staff can feel threatened by the way that resource-based learning puts more control into the hands of their students, and they may need librarians' help in adjusting to the difference in role from teacher to facilitator that may be involved.

We end this chapter with a topic that is of primary interest to academic staff, that of 'teaching-quality assessment', which they all face from time to time. Almost always, an important aspect of teaching quality is that of the range, relevance and scope of the learning resources that librarians manage in academic libraries. Reviewing learning resources provision is an opportunity for librarians to collaborate effectively with academic staff on their preparations for teaching-quality assessment, and such collaboration can be the basis for an improved understanding between librarians and academic staff. The fact that the suggestions we offer in this section are related directly to the teaching-quality procedures in England should not diminish the relevance of these suggestions to other parts of the world.

18 Liaising with academics

The simple fact about liaising with academics is that the more effort you put into it, the more effective it is. It takes you away from other tasks but, if effective, is probably the single most worthwhile activity that a subject librarian can engage in. Finding out what the information needs of your institution are at a grass roots level is critical in times of financial restraint. It allows the librarian to build up a very clear picture of what is required. The stockfund will be spent more effectively as a result, the service will probably be used more and the library will be seen as more proactive.

1. **Don't think of liaison in terms of just one academic.** Many schools have one academic who has a designated responsibility for channelling stock requests and for library liaison. This system can work well and is certainly not to be spurned, but you should be aware of its shortcomings. It is as good as the individual in harness is and does not necessarily mean that he or she will speak to all the academics in the school.

2. **Don't just liaise with academic staff!** Get to know the support staff in schools or departments too. Course administrators and faculty administrative staff can be a mine of useful information. They usually know exactly what is going on in the school or faculty, and can often fill you in on the history or background politics of a situation. They are often useful to call upon when you need to make up an interview panel too.

3. **Be aware that people may be prioritizing their own needs.** When one person represents a school or department, it may be that the system is used to ignore some areas of the

school or to build up the subject area or research interests of particular individuals.

4. **Think of liaising with all the academics in your subject area.** Even when it works well, the designated liaison academic system may only give you about 30% of what you need to know. Academics may not have (or make) the time to communicate very effectively with one another about library issues. You may be amazed at how much more you can discover on your own, by working with several academics. Of course, this may also mean that you get some conflicting requests to deal with.

5. **Don't rely too much on circulars to staff or e-mail.** Most academic staff are sinking in paperwork already. A response rate of 10% from an e-mailed circular should be regarded as good! So although librarians will get useful responses from some academics from circularized paper or electronic messages, these methods should not be relied on as primary liaison methods.

6. **Don't wait for academics to come to you.** Some will seek you out in any case, so make the most of such opportunities. However, many are rather unsure of how to go about seeking out the help of library staff, particularly in institutions where the library or learning resources centre is some distance from the areas where academic staff normally spend most of their time. It is therefore useful for library staff to make opportunities to work with academics in their own territory as well as in the library.

7. **Don't expect academics to tell you what you need from them.** The type of information we want from them is not what they carry around in the forefront of their minds. The thinking among librarians is that academics should inform them what they need to buy to service the courses – and

some do – but the fact is that most of them don't. Library operation depends on librarians knowing what is wanted, so they have to take it upon themselves to elicit from academics, and from students, the information they need.

8. **Don't blame academics.** Their priorities are simply different to ours and always will be. As a group they are busy and increasingly under pressure. The library will never be a top priority for them whether we like it or not. Librarians can be too ready to heap their frustrations about all the ills of Higher Education onto academics. This is the boring old blame game and is simply counter-productive.

9. **Go out of the library and meet them on their own territory.** As a general rule academics are always much more forthcoming on their own patch of carpet. This does, however, mean that you could be spending more time outside the library, and you may have to be ready to defend this against any colleague's reactions that you are only doing a useful job if you're slaving away at your desk!

10. **Make the most of opportunities to meet academics on neutral territory.** Useful relationships can be formed by visiting common rooms or sports facilities, and by participating in social activities in your institution, or in the departments closest to your areas of responsibility.

11. **Strike while the iron is hot!** When you have the attention of an academic you need to liaise with, don't put off till tomorrow what you can do today. The biggest waste of time is that in trying to find people, so make use of the time when you've caught up with them.

12. **Show support for your school or department.** Visit degree shows, performances by students or staff, exhibitions of work, book launches. Show a genuine interest in the *output* of the department, and avoid just being seen as 'library-

focused'. Help academic staff as much as possible through validations and teaching-quality assessments.

13. **Go to where the information you need is.** When academics are visited in their home territory – their offices – they are surrounded by the things that may be useful: the draft of the new booklist for the coming year, the latest inspection copies publishers have sent them, jottings on ideas for new courses or options etc. The vast majority of academics are also very appreciative of librarians taking the initiative. The library is immediately seen as being proactive and you become known and recognized as the librarian for the school. In short you give the library a human face.

14. **Be aware of when you might be intruding.** While you have to develop the chutzpah to stick your foot in the door, at the same time you have to learn to detect when you might be intruding. Academics are busy people and have a host of visitors and students passing through their offices. If there is obviously more urgent business afoot then go back another time.

15. **Seek out the shy ones.** In every school there are the academics whose presence is obvious and a group who live sheltered lives in cramped offices tucked away at the back of obscure laboratories. Learn to seek this second group out. The information you'll get from them is every bit as valuable as that you get from their more-visible colleagues.

16. **Make a point of introducing yourself to new members of staff.** Offer to show them round the library and explain what librarians can do for them. Find out what their special interests are and point out the most relevant stock to them. Find out which courses they are going to teach on, and find out their intentions about student reading. This sort of

exchange of information is all too easily missed in scheduled staff induction sessions.

17. **Have a standard list of questions.** The more librarians probe, the more academics remember. Once you have tracked them down in their offices, have a standard set of questions ready in your mind that you can deviate from as the need arises. What courses are you teaching on? What textbooks will you be using? Are you producing a booklist/course handbook? How many students are there on this module/option? How are you going to teach the course? Is there project work and if so how will it be organized?

18. **Take a booklist along.** It is often very useful to take along your annotated booklist or course guide for the particular course run by the academic you're visiting, so you can check out exactly what students are being asked to read. You will often find that briefings to students have changed or are changing. You'll find useful information of the sort 'we're not using that any more now', and 'yes, there's a new textbook I glanced at last week and we might as well use some chapters in it for the second year next semester'. All such information is useful to you.

19. **Consider carrying a cassette recorder!** If librarians have to ask lots of academics the same questions, it's easy to mix up their respective answers. Also, it takes too long to write all the answers down there and then, as their time is precious (and so is ours!). Ask them if you can use the recorder as an aide-memoire to make your notes later.

20. **Use corridors of opportunity.** Once librarians get known in the school, the corridors become an excellent place to do business. Much business in universities takes place in informal rather than formal settings, and if you can harness this it is all to the good. Seeing you may well remind academics of

something that they wanted to pass on, but may not have got round to otherwise.

21. **Listen to the moans.** The vast majority of academics are well disposed towards librarians, but in getting to know them, some real grumbles and resentments they may have with the library and its services can come to the surface. Some of these can be highly idiosyncratic, some downright cranky and some entirely justified. 'Five years ago somebody threw out the book I wrote'. 'I have been fined for a short loan book and academic staff should not be fined'. 'Why can't I have better access to the library catalogue from my desktop'? Even if there is nothing you can do about it, it may well help that they can moan about it to a member of the library staff.

22. **Keep records of all moans.** Sometimes it can be tempting to dismiss the importance of a moan, but if you find that the complaint is a common one, it may well mean that it will be worth addressing it seriously. You will then need statistics to justify any action you propose for overcoming the problem you've diagnosed.

23. **Choose your time to talk to academics.** Try to get round all academic staff and talk to them individually on a regular basis. If you can't do once a term then at least once a year. Early- to mid-September is probably an important time as they are just beginning to think about the new academic year and may even know which courses they will be teaching. They will have more time during parts of June and July, however, so check out when they are most ready to consult with you.

24. **Remember, it's not just about books or learning resources.** It is even more important to establish your own credibility with academics, as someone who can support their

teaching and who can help their students to learn effectively and efficiently.

25. **Always be on the lookout for opportunities.** Ideas which grow into something important often develop from chance encounters and conversations. A remark that 'first years have forgotten all about how to use the library catalogue by the time I give them their first essay!' could turn into a new first piece of work tied into the students' library induction day. 'We need more resources on this (distant) site' could lead to network terminals linking a cluster of resources to the site.

26. **Help academics to remember that you are a professional too!** Don't use body language or words which proclaim 'but I'm only a librarian' (and we've heard these words offered apologetically more times than we like to remember!).

27. **Flaunt your credentials!** Many librarians have degrees, higher degrees, membership of professional associations and other distinctions. Sometimes it's not as clear as it could be just how qualified they are. Clarifying such credentials (for example, names on doors, cards, desks, lists, committee membership and so on) can help you to be regarded 'more equally' by some academics (and can earn respect from students too).

19 Working with course committees

These are important, as they are part of the formal course structure and provide an opportunity to get feedback on the library from students. The most valuable parts are the report-back elements by the student representatives of each year of the course, and these are usually a list of the things which are currently bugging them. Course committees work best when student reps feel they are able to raise any issue they like. Course committees can, however, be used by academics to slap down student criticisms of the course, and these are the least productive meetings.

1. **Get involved with course committees.** It is best that you start your involvement even before a new course reaches validation, as this can help you to make sure that library resources are flagged as an important issue, and planned for accordingly, well before the course comes to implementation.

2. **The most important thing is that you are present and listening to what is said.** You don't have to worry about making any speeches. An important part of your role is to listen to what academics and students have to say, and to pick up any new information.

3. **Read the advance paperwork carefully.** Look out for items on the agenda which may involve the library, and do your own research on the issues involved, so that you will be able to make useful and informed contributions at the meeting.

4. **Try to get library matters down as a regular agenda item.** This can save you time. Much of the business may not be directly relevant to you, and having a 'library' agenda item

can give more focus to the discussion. Even so it is a good idea to stay around to hear the student reps, as they tend to remember more items that may relate to the library role as they go along.

5.   **Use the committees to get to know key players.** Course committees are likely to be your best way of building a relationship with course leaders and maybe heads of department. Even if you don't agree with them, you can work more effectively with them when you know how their minds work.

6.   **Recognize the vociferous minority.** They may not reflect general opinion, and it can be destructive to bow too much to their demands. When necessary, clarify how widespread particular views are by asking for a vote or show of hands, or ask for feedback on how many members of the committee agree/disagree with proposals or resolutions.

7.   **Don't expect praise.** Even when you know you've done a good job for the course concerned, committees tend not to award bouquets. It is better to use such committees as occasions when you can tune in to people's feelings and impressions about the workings of the library, and look for actions that you can initiate to solve some of the problems you may hear about.

8.   **Encourage criticism.** What you want is for the students to tell you what is on their minds and the best way to do this is to encourage them to moan. Don't worry if this starts to happen since this is one of the purposes of course committees. Also, academics expect to be able to add their criticisms of the library on such occasions.

9.   **Divide the issues raised between those you can do something about and those you can't.** Problems over which you have no control may be raised time and time again. There may be vociferous complaints about the cost of photo-

copying – the price of which may fixed by the institution. Students or staff may want you to open the library on Sundays – you may have no staff to do this. You can only note such issues down as desirable and report that they have been raised.

10. **Take particular note of the issues you may be able to change.** It's important that you will be in a position to report back to your own colleagues exactly what these issues are, and let them know how the issue was ranked in importance by staff and students.

11. **Develop your role in the committee.** Gradually make it a more proactive one. Become identified as part of the course team, and get involved in discussions about approaches to learning.

12. **Be able to explain why things can't be done.** What may be desirable for one group may not be possible or appropriate for the library service as a whole. While you won't want to appear as a 'wet blanket' when requests are made, it is important not to raise unrealistic hopes when it is just not viable to implement something that a course committee may be seeking.

13. **Don't promise without knowing that you can deliver.** You can promise to *address* a problem, without at that stage giving your commitment regarding the nature of the solution that may be found, or indeed guaranteeing that a solution can be found.

14. **Don't stop when the meeting does!** You can often do productive business after the meeting has finished. Sometimes there will be things you may have wanted to say during the meeting, but which can more usefully be said after the meeting to the one or two people directly affected, rather than taking up everyone's time. Also, if there are students present

at the meeting, you may be able to get them together for a few minutes after the meeting for a short brainstorm of suggestions for the stock.

15. **Write notes upon which to base your report straight away.** If you're involved in several course committees and there is a cluster of meetings within a day or two, it's easy for events and issues from one meeting to get mixed up with other meetings!

16. **File your own notes, as well as any formal reports you write about each meeting.** Sometimes it will be politic to phrase formal reports gently or somewhat vaguely, and you may need to resort to your own notes to remind yourself of who was involved in making strong criticisms or who had useful ideas.

17. **Make sure that your successes are well-minuted.** Teaching-quality assessors, for example, may well go through the issues raised in course committee minutes, and it is important to make sure that the changes you were able to make as a result of suggestions made in the meetings are recorded clearly.

20 Working with educational development colleagues

There is much in common between the work of the educational or staff developer and that of librarians; both roles have strong emphasis on increasing the quality of students' learning. It is useful to develop a healthy relationship with the people in your college who are involved with staff development. The following suggestions may help.

1. **Be useful to your educational developers.** Make sure that the library stock includes key texts and journals that will be useful to educational developers, and to the people they work with. Ask them to recommend texts and packages that might be useful.

2. **Educational development spans the whole operation of the college.** Books on teaching and learning are relevant to staff and students from all faculties or departments. This means that the provision of these should not just come out of the budget for individual departments, but ideally out of a central pool. It is also useful to ensure that stock on teaching and learning development is not hidden away within the stacks relating to individual disciplines.

3. **Get to know your educational developers.** Invite them to help you to design and run library induction sessions for new staff. Work with them in the parts of such programmes which relate to library familiarization. Seek their advice about, and contributions to, your own induction programmes for students.

4. **Join in with feedback-seeking initiatives.** Educational development colleagues are often involved in gathering or

analysing student feedback on courses and on other services including library provision. The sort of feedback librarians can get by working closely with them is well worth having.

5. **Get your educational developers to run workshops for library staff.** They will be pleased to share with library colleagues (for example) recent developments in teaching styles, or ideas on helping students to develop independent learning skills. Such workshops are an excellent way of helping educational developers to get to know a wide cross-section of library staff, rather than just the librarians most closely connected with teaching and learning development.

6. **Get into educational development across the institution.** One of the best ways of going about this is to ensure that library staff are always represented at staff development and training workshops, whether college-wide ones or department-based ones. Once in there, make sure that library staff participation is useful and valued, and not seen as a nuisance.

7. **Offer to provide elements to educational development workshops.** For example, in a training session on resource-based learning, it can be very useful to the facilitator when someone from the library can bring along a selection of resource materials for participants to inspect, and also give a short presentation about the features that make for good learning resources.

8. **Try to get included in educational development planning.** It can be useful to have a library representative on the team or committee that plans the college educational development programme, and on committees leading particular developments such as implementing flexible learning or developing computer-based assessment.

9. **Pass on business to your educational developers.** Library staff often are the first to know when teaching staff are having problems with their teaching. Build up the sort of relationship where you can counsel academic colleagues about how valuable it may be for them to go and have a chat with a named educational developer, who you know will be able to offer direct support.

10. **Coorganize joint events.** Open days, conferences, training events, workshops and seminars can provide a chance for educational developers and librarians to collaborate in productive ways, particularly in demonstrating the effectiveness of IT-based packages and open learning materials.

11. **Set up a joint resource centre.** Work with educational developers to produce a collection of books, resources, TLTP* packages, videos, tapes and other items to promote effective teaching and learning among academics. A good example is MARCET (Materials and Resources Centre for Education and Technology) at the University of Northumbria at Newcastle.

---

*TLTP is 'Teaching and Learning Technology Programme' an initiative in the UK where special funding was awarded to projects to promote the use of technology in teaching and learning.

21 Encouraging academics to use resource-based learning effectively

Academic staff are keen to use new methods of curriculum delivery, not only because they may be more cost-effective but also because they may be powerful enhancers of learning. The librarian has a key role in helping colleagues to move from a tutor-centred mode of teaching towards student-centred learning in which learning resources play a large part.

1. **Help them to identify what they've got already.** Learning resources often have quite simple origins: a lecturer's course notes can fairly readily be transformed into learning materials with some rewriting and improved presentation.

2. **Dissuade them from simply dumping their notes on the Web!** Some lecturers are so keen to make use of the new technologies available that they want to put everything they've got up on the World Wide Web. Although it can be of benefit to have course notes placed there, there is an art to writing Web pages that are readable. Librarians may not be able to prevent lecturers from making inappropriate use of the Web, but may be able to influence the development of an institutional policy on such practices: flagging up the complexities of copyright issues may help.

3. **Raid their bookshelves!** Academics often have vast amounts of useful learning resources sitting around on shelves in their offices, lying unused for months on end. Help them to liberate these private collections and place them where they can be of more use.

4. **Help them to work out how best to use library stock.** The way set-text books and short term loan items are used can radically influence the effectiveness of resource-based learning, and academics don't always understand the complexities of this.

5. **Advise them about copyright.** This is a complex area in relation to resource-based learning. You could direct them to the copyright section of the Course Design for Resource-Based Learning series by Graham Gibbs et al, (see list of further reading), or the more comprehensive Library Association Copyright Guide *Copyright in further and higher education libraries*.

6. **Help them to network internally.** Often lecturers are trying to instigate resource-based learning within their courses without knowing that others in their universities are further down the line from them and in a position to offer advice and support. Help them to make contact with one another.

7. **Help them to network externally.** Library staff often know of developments in other institutions, and can pass on to lecturers names of colleagues who may have developed or adapted useful learning resources.

8. **Remind lecturers about the importance of effective learning.** It's easy to become blinded by the gloss and sophistication of some learning resource materials, and to forget to look critically enough at whether the materials actually deliver the learning payoff which is sought. Suggest to lecturers that they continue to ask students how well they learn from each different resource, and to test the learning outcomes appropriately.

9. **Encourage lecturers to play with new learning resources.** Sometimes you will have the opportunity to introduce a new learning package to lecturers who you know are

involved in teaching the subject concerned. It can be very effective simply to let them see, in the relative comfort of privacy, what the materials can do.

10. **Help lecturers to evaluate resources.** For example, give them an exercise to do in the learning resources centre, such as 'compile a guide for students on the learning resources relating to your module', then give them feedback on the product of their exercise, and maybe help them to get it produced in a suitable format for issue to students.

11. **Don't forget to help students too.** When new forms of learning resource materials are adopted by lecturers and located in the library, it's often the case that students need some extra guidance about how to make the most of the learning packages concerned. Being watchful and available until students get the hang of it is very helpful to all concerned.

12. **Opportunity to help decreases as demand increases.** It can be worth getting everyone involved in resource-based learning together from time to time, to check the sorts of help that staff and students are needing most, and to discuss ways of streamlining the provision of help.

22 Preparing for quality assessments

Libraries and computing services are among the facilities looked at by teams visiting institutions for the purposes of teaching-quality assessments. Many parts of this book contain suggestions that relate to such inspections, but we believe it will be useful to collect together here some of the most relevant aspects of provision that are likely to be the focus during such visits. Because of the close connections between many aspects of library, learning resource centre, and computer services provision, we have combined our discussion of all of these below. The following suggestions are based on recommendations drawn together in the UK by the Standing Conference of National and University Librarians (SCONUL) and the Universities and Colleges Information Systems Association (UCISA) together with the teaching-quality assessment division of HEFCE.

1. **Check the connections between library and computer services to course development and review.** It is particularly useful to review these links in the specific context of the disciplines to be covered by a forthcoming teaching-quality assessment. It helps a great deal if it can be shown quite clearly that there are representatives from the library and computer services on the course boards involved in the quality assessment, and particularly at review and validation events.

2. **Work with the course teams in the preparation of their self-assessment documents.** In the teaching-quality assessment systems currently used in the UK, the agenda for assessment visits is strongly dependent upon the content of

the self-assessment document produced by the schools or departments involved in the inspection. It is therefore important for library staff to be fully aware of what has been claimed in the self-assessment document regarding the specific provision which links to the courses being assessed.

3. **Avoid the temptation to grumble to the quality assessors!** While they may be very receptive to the difficulties that the library staff encounter in trying to provide for the staff and students on the courses they are quality-assessing, a poor outcome of the quality assessment visit will benefit no-one.

4. **Appoint one person to be in charge of the library's representation during each teaching-quality assessment visit.** It is important that there is someone who can take overall responsibility for ensuring that on the occasion of a teaching-quality assessment visit, the visitors will be shown all the resources and facilities that are directly relevant to the courses or programmes being assessed.

5. **Ensure that everyone is fully briefed for the occasion of a quality assessment visit.** The visitors will probably spend a limited amount of time in the library, but it is important to ensure that this time is spent well, and on matters directly relating to the staff and students on the courses being quality-assessed on that occasion. Librarians may also be called in to meetings with the teaching-quality assessors in the department being visited.

6. **Library and computer services staff need to be seen to communicate together effectively.** In institutions where the services have already been combined, this should not pose any problems. However, problems have been known when the services have remained separate, for example when different specifications and standards of computing

equipment are used in the respective departments. Teaching-quality assessors are likely to notice any tensions between different parts of the provision supporting the courses they are investigating.

7. **Be prepared to show that library staff communicate effectively with the academic staff teaching the courses being assessed.** Teaching-quality assessors are likely to talk to both teaching staff and support staff, and will notice quickly if there are any discrepancies in the information they receive from each source. It is best to be able to demonstrate clear mechanisms whereby support service staff are kept aware of the requirements on them, such as in changing courses.

8. **Have clear open lines of communication between students and library staff and computer services staff.** Student feedback plays an important role in quality enhancement of academic programmes, and is equally important to ensure that libraries, learning resource centres and computing services function well. Teaching-quality assessors will be keen to check that the students on the programmes they are assessing have good opportunities to provide feedback on the provision they encounter.

9. **Ensure that students are actively encouraged to make full use of the facilities available to them in libraries and computing centres.** It is often the case that students are so busy trying to keep up to date with their coursework and assessments that they do not know the range of help and facilities available to them in libraries and computing centres. It is useful for library staff to be seen to inform students about the resources at their disposal and encourage them in their use.

10. **Be prepared to show that new academic staff are given useful induction into the library and computing provi-**

sion. While it can be useful for them to have a short talk by a senior member of the library and the computing service, this only really serves to give them one or two faces they may remember. It is better to include a short tour of the facilities as part of staff induction programmes.

11. **Library and computing support needs to be seen to match course requirements, as outlined in the self-assessment document produced by the course team.** Teaching-quality assessors are likely to probe whether the resources are sufficient in quantity and appropriate in quality for students on the courses being assessed.

12. **Have clear and appropriate mechanisms for the selection of relevant learning resource materials and equipment.** It is important to show that library staff are fully involved with academic staff in the choices and purchases of the learning resource materials underpinning delivery of the courses being quality-assessed. The systems by which teaching staff are involved in the most appropriate selection of materials may need to be checked and improved, especially where budgets are tight and hard decisions have to be made..

13. **Check that the availability of facilities and resources is sufficient, as far as possible, to match student needs on the courses being quality-assessed.** Desk collections, or reference-only stock are ways of coping with high student demand for particular resources. With computing equipment, tracking the usage and availability of terminals and machines is an important step towards trying to meet demand and extend the opportunities for students to use equipment.

14. **Ensure that the pressures on library study space are monitored.** It is important to be able to show that every attempt has been made to make sufficient space available to

the particular student groups on the courses being quality-assessed, particularly towards examinations time.

15. **User-support needs to be seen to be available to both students and staff on the courses being quality-assessed.** Do a survey of the skills-training available for effective use of the library and the computing facilities. Help-desks and help-lines are a visible sign of such support, and feedback should be gathered about how effective the training and support is in practice. In particular, it is important to be able to show that those members of library staff with direct connections to the courses being quality-assessed are involved in meeting the specific needs of the academic staff and students involved in these courses, rather than just to present a general picture of an adequate level of overall institutional support.

16. **Help academic staff to ask for the specific support they need.** Sometimes staff are embarrassed to ask for help from more junior staff or if students are around, because they don't want to look foolish. Develop sensitive mechanisms where seeking support doesn't call attention to the user, and ensure that the staff involved in the courses being quality-assessed are given particular attention in the context of the forthcoming quality assessment.

17. **Ensure that appropriate support is available to all groups of students on the courses being quality-assessed.** Library and computing facilities and support need to be suitable not only to the full-time students working on the courses involved but also to students who are studying part-time, or by distance learning programmes.

18. **Library staff training programmes are an indicator of the intention to achieve quality enhancement.** All computing and library staff should have opportunities to partici-

pate in relevant and appropriate staff development activities, and the effectiveness of these should be monitored. It is useful to be able to demonstrate that the library staff involved in supporting the courses being quality-assessed are actively participating in such training.

19. **Be seen to be in a position to advise staff on how to spend their money.** This is more a matter for the computing support services than for the library, but often the two run together in such matters. Academic staff who buy computer equipment may not be completely *au fait* with the technology, and costly mistakes can be made by making unwise or inappropriate purchasing decisions. Some institutions only permit purchases of IT equipment through central agencies, which can be frustrating for individuals, but can enable good cost savings through negotiated contracts with suppliers, and can ensure informed decisions. It can be useful to show to quality assessors that staff are well advised.

20. **Don't forget that quality enhancement applies to many other services.** In a book of this kind, it would be impossible for us to go into factors relating quality assessment to (for example) media services, learning resource production services, television studio provision, student services, accommodation services and so on, as such provision is usually organized in very different ways in different institutions. However, in the context of teaching-quality assessment visits, it can be useful for the representatives of each of the services involved to be seen to be pulling together effectively in the context of the claims about support made in the self-assessment document.

Chapter 5
Looking after yourself

So far in this book, we have tended to focus on the needs of our institutions, and those of the students and staff making up the main profile of academic library users. At last, in this chapter, we turn towards the needs and aspirations of librarians themselves.

We start with some suggestions on managing your time. If you are feeling pressurized in the context of your workload, we hope you will find something in our suggestions to bring you some practical help. We move next to the related topic of managing stress. We don't take the view that all causes of stress should be, or could be, abolished, but rather that there are ways of developing coping strategies which will enable you look after yourself even in situations that are somewhat stressful.

Our next section is entitled 'Dealing with complaints'. No-one in a service provision can hope to abolish complaints, and indeed they are one form of the feedback upon which librarians can base aspirations for the improvement and development of their provision. That said, each and every complaint is likely to be regarded as highly important by the complainant, and we trust that our suggestions may give you some ideas on how to handle complaints in ways that lead to each party being satisfied.

We move next to some thoughts about personal safety. It is improbable that your personal safety would be threatened in the normal conduct of your work, but there are occasions when this can be a possibility, and it can give some assurance to have considered the issues involved beforehand.

Our attention is turned next to 'Giving critical feedback to colleagues'. This is always a sensitive area, and we hope that our suggestions will help towards creating a climate in your library where any such criticism is given honestly, openly, and in a caring and sensitive way.

We end this chapter with a topic that is a major problem to many colleagues, yet not one which need involve deep emotions: that of 'Handling paperwork'! In one sense, much of the job of a librarian is likely to involve paperwork, so the secret is to help colleagues to get in charge of their paperwork, rather than leading to them feeling that they are victims to it.

23 Managing your time

Academic librarians, contrary to public opinion, have hectic lives and it is easy to feel, in a job where people are making demands on you at all times of the day, that you never have a moment to yourself. The following tips won't magically transform your life but they may make it possible for you to manage your time more effectively.

1. **Plan ahead long term.** It doesn't really matter whether you use a wall chart, a diary, a personal organizer or day/week planner book or file, so long as you have a clear system for logging and tracking your activities and commitments.

2. **Plan ahead short term too.** Librarians lives often revolve around timetables, prepared a week or so in advance, dealing with the staffing of service points. Make sure that you get a list of your other commitments to the person doing the timetabling, well in advance. If you need to be at a meeting in another institution, it is best for this to be planned into everyone's work, rather than you having to try and find someone to swap rosters with.

3. **Be willing to do things at almost zero notice.** Even with the best planning possible, people can be off sick, and timetables have to be rearranged to cope with such contingencies. Help out whenever you can, rather than trying to resist such last-minute changes to your plans. If you're known for normally being someone who will take on last-minute changes, people will be more understanding on occasions when you can't do this because of important commitments.

4. **Prioritize your tasks.** For each job in hand, ask yourself whether it is urgent or non-urgent and important or not

important. If it is urgent and important, do it straight away and do it well. If it is not urgent but important, block in some time in your schedule to make a decent job of it. If it is urgent but not important, deal with it quickly but don't invest too much energy in it, and if it's not urgent or important either throw it away or put it into a file for jobs to do when you are bored or have nothing much else to do.

5.   **Reserve a time every week to plan your workload.** Some people find it easiest to do this on a Friday afternoon, so they can come in at the start of the week organized for action. Find your own best time, perhaps during a quiet time of the week (if any) when you are likely to be uninterrupted, so you can read through papers for meetings coming up, update your working log, map out your urgent and important tasks.

6.   **Break big jobs down into little jobs.** Sometimes there just seems to be too much to do and so it's difficult to see the wood for the trees. Don't allow yourself to be daunted by huge tasks. It is often useful to break a huge task up into small elements, and then just tackle one small part. The first job might just be listing what you have to do!

7.   **Do it now!** Undertake one relatively small defined task when you have an hour or two available and try to complete it within the time, so that you can see small but steady progress.

8.   **Limit your time.** If you are likely to spend too much time on something you enjoy, carry out some other tasks first, and constrain the time available for the activity that could swallow more time than would be reasonable.

9.   **Bunch your tasks.** Try to do all your phone calls in one go, so that if you don't get a reply you can move straight on to the next one. Similarly collect paperwork and filing, e-mail or

photocopying together. It is often quicker to do several of these small tasks at a time than to butterfly from one job to another.

10. **Use the most efficient medium.** If you need to talk to someone it is tempting just to pop across and see them, and there can be great value in these kinds of social interaction. However, if you are busy, it is usually faster to phone and faster still to fax or e-mail.

11. **Don't time-manage people out altogether.** Some things are faster and more successful with the right face-to-face contacts, body language, facial expressions, and social exchanges, so make sure that you don't lose important social opportunities in your bid to save time. Sometimes, you've got to invest in some time getting to know people well, to save time in the long run.

12. **De-demonize your phone!** Don't let it rule your life and try to make parts of your day phone-free if you have big tasks on the go. If you are able, negotiate with a colleague to take your calls for an hour or so and reciprocate when they are busy. Within the limits of your job, consider the use of answer-phones or voice mail to free you from the tyranny of the phone for short periods.

13. **Use down-time constructively.** Sometimes in the middle of a major task you feel bored, or on occasions you will have half an hour or so before your next commitment. Save up little unimportant tasks to do in these flat periods and get a great glow of satisfaction from crossing them off your list!

14. **Can you delegate anything?** Is there any part of your workload that you can pass on (by negotiation) to a colleague? But be careful not to pass on your problems by delegating to someone who is also busy but can't refuse. The best person to be delegated to isn't always the most junior.

24 Managing stress

Outsiders may have visions of library staff working in a quiet environment, with time to read books, and with little stress. While there is not the life-or-death kind of stress as found in the lives of surgeons or steeplejacks, the job of an academic librarian can be stressful, and there are not always well-defined procedures that can be followed in difficult circumstances. You will need to find your own ways of coping with everything from minor traumas to major catastrophes. The following suggestions may help you find how to start with these.

1. **Just say no!** Stress is often piled onto librarians by people giving them things to do that are not really their responsibility. Learning to say 'no' to things that you are just too busy to do is really difficult, especially since librarians' jobs entail helping people all the time. What you may need to learn to do is to say 'no' firmly, politely, offering alternative suggestions where possible but without apologizing.

2. **Let other people know what you are doing.** Put your work schedule or lists of your current urgent, medium term and long term tasks on the wall by your work area for all to see, and you make your workload explicit. When someone wants to give you a new task, you can then negotiate as to where it will fit into your schedule and people will (or should) recognize that you have other demands made on your time than theirs alone.

3. **Look after yourself:** you need to find ways within your job and outside it to de-stress yourself, whether it is through exercise, relaxation or gossiping! Doing something physical helps many people to get the aggravations of life out of their system.

4. **Get better at recognizing the signs of stress.** Stress creeps up on most people, and you can't start your coping strategies if you aren't aware that you may need to. Waking up in the early hours worrying about work-related matters, is not normal behaviour for people who have no stress in their lives! People who become really stressed are often those who won't talk about how they feel or who try to cope for too long on their own without asking for help.

5. **Remember to have a lunch break!** It is important to look after yourself in basic ways like this. Get away from the library if possible. You will be more productive in the afternoon than if you yielded to temptations or pressures to skip lunch. The same goes for tea-breaks and coffee-breaks. One reason why people have breaks is because they work better when they have them.

6. **Be realistic:** some research suggests that people don't get stressed because they have a lot to do, but more because they are worried about whether the time they have available is sufficient to do it in. Don't be too tough on yourself by having unrealistic expectations of what you can do.

7. **Make lists.** For example, at the start of a day make a list of the things you want to try to achieve that day (not that year!). Often, you'll be surprised how once you can see all the items, you're better able to tackle any one of them, secure that you haven't got to keep remembering everything on the list any more.

8. **Employ work-avoidance tactics deliberately!** For example, if there's a job that you're a bit stressed about, do something entirely different – something short – first. This gives your mind time to get prepared for the more daunting task.

9. **Analyse the causes of stress.** When you've got time to do some gentle analysis, work out what it is exactly about a

task, or about a person, that actually seems to cause you stress. Then you may feel that not everything about it or them stresses you, just one or two identified things, and that is easier to cope with.

10. **Adjust your ergonomics!** Take a little time to rearrange your desk or work station. It is so easy to fall into postural habits that leave you aching and sore at the end of the day. Think about chair heights, foot rests, and the angle that your monitor screen is tilted at. Sometimes we have good equipment, but manage to use it quite badly.

11. **Give yourself a few minutes to unwind after a busy counter session.** One of the problems with staffing a service point is that everyone wants something or needs something as fast as we can cope with them. We therefore get into the habit of coping with their needs as fast as we can. But we sometimes forget to stop rushing when there is no reason to hurry any more.

12. **Do some problem solving.** When a problem stresses you, work out exactly what the problem is, then check out whether it's really *your* problem, or whether in fact it belongs to someone else. People in general spend far too long worrying about problems that aren't actually theirs to solve.

13. **Try a negative brainstorm.** If something stresses you, try to imagine three ways that the stress could be made even worse. Doing this often gives useful clues as to how the stress could in fact be reduced, by doing the opposite of the stress-increasing actions.

14. **Remember to delegate.** It often seems easier to do something yourself than to explain to someone what needs doing. However, if you never delegate such things, you'll just end up doing them yourself repeatedly, adding to your stress levels.

15. **Have a friend who knows your work situation.** This can be a colleague, or a relative or friend. When you are under stress, it is essential to have someone who knows enough about your work situation to allow you to confide in them. Just the act of explaining your situation to someone else helps you clarify it for yourself.

16. **Meet people in the 'real' world.** It is important in any job to avoid the job becoming too great a part of your life and of your view of the world. It is fine to have friends at work, but the danger is that relaxation time can get taken over by talking shop. We all need someone now and then to chide us 'Good heavens, and you're worrying about *that*?!'.

17. **Accept the right to feel stressed.** Don't pretend it's something that should never happen to you, or that it's a weakness on your part. It is perfectly normal human behaviour to get stressed under various circumstances. Indeed, it can be argued that if we have too little stress, we are in danger of sinking into lassitude and boredom. A complete absence of stress is not our goal, it is better to look at ways of coping with some stress. Acknowledging that one is feeling stressed is often a useful first step towards countering the causes of the stress.

25 Dealing with complaints

Every service sector must expect to deal with dissatisfied users, and libraries are no different in this respect from shops or other public services. This set of suggestions aims to help you to resolve problem issues in ways that will defuse the situation and remedy errors and deficiencies.

1. **Listen to the complaint.** When a user has a grievance of some description, it is very important to hear the complaint out and establish what the facts are. Do not assume that the library will be in the right: mistakes will have been made in the past and will continue to be made. Establishing the facts of a case is something that librarians can do in a calm and objective way.

2. **Apologize and get down to the nub of the problem.** Very often, what angry people really want is your time and attention. If you think they have a genuine grievance, or have fallen foul of the system in some way, address their problems. Once the person feels that progress is being made, even if you can't completely satisfy them there and then, their anger will start to disperse. It is always a challenge to see if you can turn a disaffected user into one who thinks well of your service.

3. **Go the extra mile.** If somebody has genuinely fallen foul of the system for whatever reason, go a little further than you normally would in helping them. Smoothing things over creates good will and your complainant may well go away singing your praises.

4. **Don't blame the user ill-advisedly.** Be sure of your own ground before you pass back the problem to the user. If you

are absolutely sure that you are right, try to state this calmly and non-confrontationally. No-one likes to be told that they're wrong in so many words, even when they know that they are wrong.

5. **Try to avoid making the complaint into a public spectacle.** Sit the user down and try to make it into a conversation rather than an argument. Without risking your personal safety, consider taking the complainant into a quiet space to discuss the matter.

6. **Calm the situation by referring the user on.** If a member of staff does get into a confrontation with a user, and becomes locked into a battle of wills, it usually helps to defuse the situation if another person takes over. People seem to be more ready to deal with someone who has come out of an office. It does not matter whether that person is a superior or not, people seem impressed by those who inhabit the space behind the public area.

7. **Let the complainant make the case.** Hear what they have to say, listening attentively. If possible, let them explain the problem as fully as they wish so that they don't feel silenced or ignored. Then ask questions to check that you understand the situation properly, and make proposals to put things right. Ensure that you do what you say you are going to do.

8. **Offer remedies.** Make sure before the situation becomes critical that you have listened to the complainant's case and looked at what you can do about it. Don't go immediately onto the defensive, as this can spark confrontation.

9. **Try to find a compromise.** People generally want to see their dispute settled, but also want to save face. We also want to solve any problems with our systems or procedures, and want to see that justice is done. We also want, and need, the

goodwill of users; getting this is not served by point scoring or exacting revenge.

10. **Know what your bottom line is.** It is also possible to go too far towards accommodating wrong-doers. If you do this, you tend to encourage further rule-breaking. If they get away with it once, they may try it again. It is also unfair to those library users who do abide by the rules. It is important to know what is negotiable, and what is not.

26 Looking after your personal safety

It's a fact of life, however unwelcome, that librarians may encounter aggressive and violent behaviour in an academic library. Despite the fact that your employer has a legal duty to devise and maintain safe working practices, by what ever means, to keep you safe, there are some contingencies that cannot be planned for. The following tips are designed to help you to take sensible precautions and to look after yourself if the worst were to happen.

1. **Take care of yourself.** It's your legal responsibility to take reasonable care for your own, and others' safety, so try to avoid getting into unpleasant circumstances in the first place.

2. **Defuse situations.** If you are confronted with aggression, try to speak calmly and don't rise to the bait. Anger faced with anger often escalates. Listen to any grievances and complaints and try to answer them without being self-excusing or confrontational.

3. **Share information about regular users who cause problems.** Knowing whom to keep an eye on is useful, and also knowing how best to respond to these particular people can save a lot of time and trouble.

4. **Think about your body language.** If someone looks as though they are about to become violent, your body language may give suggestions that you are going to defend yourself, and this can provoke an instinctive attack. Of course, be as ready as you can to defend yourself, but try not to admit to this state through your body language: the fact that you look

unabashed by the threat may well diminish the probability of violence.

5. **Avoid adopting a tense, aggressive body posture.** An aggressor could mirror this, and their arousal could increase. Keep your distance, and avoid face-to-face confrontation.

6. **Think about the language you use.** Saying 'Now look here' or 'Don't be ridiculous!' might make matters worse, whereas 'I can see why that might be upsetting' or 'Let's see if we can find a way to work this out' is likely to be more helpful. Try to sound helpful, reassuring and confident.

7. **Think about your voice.** Even though you may be terrified, try to keep your voice calm, conversational, even-toned and reassuring. Never shout back, as this can cause the aggression to escalate.

8. **Think about the aggressor.** Be aware that the person concerned may be upset, frightened, confused, or may not understand the situation. Treat the aggressor as a person, and don't assume that reason and common sense are pointless.

9. **Give your confronter a chance to speak.** Keep your counsel and hear the person out: just listening may be enough to calm the situation.

10. **Weigh up whether to ask the aggressor to desist.** Sometimes asking the aggressor to stop will work, often to the relief of both parties. Otherwise, you can ask the person to leave, and sometimes the act of leaving noisily with a slammed door can be enough for the aggressor.

11. **Have contingency plans.** If you are likely to be working alone, with responsibility for an area of the library, make sure you know the emergency phone numbers needed to get help, and how to get out in the worst possible scenario.

12. **If things still don't improve after trying out the appropriate suggestions from above, get out yourself.** There's no point in heroics if you are putting your personal safety at risk. In the final analysis, if by leaving you are putting no-one else at risk, it may be the wisest course of action.

13. **Don't wait to ask for help.** If the situation is getting out of hand, use a panic button, or use the phone or call a colleague over. Avoid shouting, if possible, as this may inflame an aggressor. Don't feel, however, that you will lose face by not being able to handle conflict on your own.

14. **Don't necessarily send in the heavies!** In the case of a fully fledged attack, it makes sense for the strongest or most physically able person to intervene. However, if the situation is only potentially threatening, confrontation may be avoided by using a less-threatening figure to defuse the situation.

15. **Keep a watchful eye out.** Be vigilant for signs of likely aggression, without being paranoid. Be sensitive to unusual behaviour, without letting your anxiety become a self-fulfilling prophesy.

16. **Don't take on what you can't handle.** Don't try to break up fights, where the perpetrators might turn on you, and don't take responsibility for what you are not trained to handle. Look after the safety of bystanders, and call in experts to take care of violence wherever possible.

27 Giving critical feedback to colleagues

Telling someone that their performance is not up to scratch or that you don't think that someone is responsible enough, are among the hardest things you can ever do. That is why we've put our suggestions on this in the 'Looking after yourself' chapter (we hope you will also be looking after your criticized colleagues).

1. **Try not to criticize a fellow human being!** It is much safer – and kinder – to criticize something someone has done than to criticize the person who has done it.

2. **Don't wait until you've got a whole raft of critical comments to make.** It's only too easy to let things slip, while gradually storing up resentment, and then to explode with little warning. It is worth trying to pick a single area to address critical feedback towards, and to do it straight away, and to defer all the other matters till another time.

3. **Try to get the people themselves to identify what is wrong.** This saves you having to tell them what is wrong. If people feel a sense of ownership of a problem, they are much more ready to explore with you approaches towards solving the problem.

4. **When you need to give critical feedback, plan the time and place.** It is normally best done when you can prepare the words and approaches you will use calmly and quietly, rather than hurriedly or publicly. Allow time for a satisfactory resolution of the problem to be arrived at and agreed.

5. **Do not criticize an individual in front of colleagues.** Such happenings may never be forgotten, and can sour rela-

tionships permanently. When it is necessary, take the individual aside, preferably into private, comfortable surroundings, and make sure that both of you are seated before you embark on the criticism.

6. **Agree a course of action to remedy the problem.** If it is difficult to reach agreement yourselves, agree who may be brought in to help, for example someone from personnel or welfare with appropriate skills and training.

7. **Watch carefully the body language of the person you are criticizing.** Some people take criticism relatively boldly and easily; others become so anxious or defensive that the critical feedback never really reaches home. Adjust your approach as you continue, accommodating the reactions you see. Don't get into the position of having to say (as one social worker we know did) 'But I didn't notice you were in tears.'

8. **Don't make threats you won't, or can't, carry out.** If you have to give someone a warning, it is better to explain the various courses of action that could be chosen if the situation were to arise again.

9. **Continue to be ready to listen.** Quite often, when we hear the other side of a situation, the critical feedback we may need to give is softened or even vanishes. Giving the other person their say helps them to feel that they are being treated fairly and justly.

10. **Consider the possibility of giving critical feedback in a neutral situation.** For example, it is often possible to be critical of a situation while talking to a group of people, when the feedback is really only directed at one of them. This avoids having to point the finger directly, but can still have the desired effect. However, balance this against the possibility of demotivating other staff, whom you are not intending to criticize.

11. **Take at least some ownership of problems.** Suppose, for example, you need to give some critical feedback following a complaint by Dr Smith. Starting off by saying 'I'm having a hard time with Dr Smith because of...', may be a better way into a discussion than saying 'Dr Smith says you aren't doing your job properly'.

12. **When necessary, cover your back!** There are times when you'll need to prove that you acted fairly and appropriately, and it may be useful to have witnesses to a difficult interview, or paperwork showing what was discussed and what decisions were reached.

28 Handling paperwork

Paperwork is the bane of the academic librarian's life. It is easy to feel that we are drowning in paper, and that's just when individual key documents misplace themselves. If you follow all these tips you will be a paragon of perfection (unlike the authors) and you will make life much easier for yourself.

1. **A place for everything...!** Obvious, but true. Time is often wasted looking for things, and a well organized system can make life much easier. It's always a chore to do routine filing, but making sure that your papers and files are sensibly located will make all the difference when you are in a hurry.

2. **Try to handle each piece of paper as few times as possible.** Often you will look at letters, memos, reports and other things that pass across your desk a number of times before you actually deal with them. As an exercise, put a pencil mark in the corner of the paper each time you look at it, and when the marks become a forest this will give you a strong cue that you need to do something with it!

3. **Give yourself stark choices.** Most documents have one of three destinations: the bin, the filing tray or the out tray. As far as you can, deal with small tasks immediately and get them on their way to their next destination promptly. This leaves your work station less cluttered for your major tasks.

4. **Be ruthless.** Throw away immediately everything that you can see no use for, and radically review your filing cabinet at least annually. Don't wait until you move offices before you get out the black bin bags! You will be amazed at how much rubbish you have kept for years and will find that anything really important is usually retrievable from another source.

(If it isn't don't throw it away, because you can guarantee that if you do, you will need it in the next week!)

5. **Keep an indefinite pending file.** Keep it out of sight in a drawer and put into it anything you don't quite know what to do with or think you might need some day. Once it has sat in the drawer for a year or two you can be reasonably certain that you won't need it again and you can throw it away.

6. **Get yourself a nine-part organizer.** This is a file with multiple sections and an elastic strap to stop papers falling out. Put into this all the papers you will need for different sections of the day (minutes of meetings you will attend, relevant correspondence), one set of papers per section. This way you don't have to lug whole files around with you and you look wonderfully organized as you turn up with the right papers at each of your meetings through the day.

7. **Keep off irrelevant mailing lists.** Only receive publicity material that you are really going to read. Don't hoard all the items that you receive from such lists as most of it, for example newsletters, book lists and so on, goes out of date within months.

8. **Throw out old catalogues the minute you get new ones.** It is much faster to look up books in publishers' catalogues when you only have the current one and you don't have to waste extra minutes finding the right catalogue.

9. **Be particularly careful with invoices.** Pass them on as soon as possible. Great embarrassment is caused when they get found under piles of paperwork six months later!

10. **Don't keep hard copy when you have secure electronic versions.** Don't feel that you always have to keep a paper version of every document you send out. The authors know of one university where purchase orders for filing cabinets

are no longer approved, in a bid to persuade staff not to keep too much paper. (There is, however, a thriving internal trade in second-hand ones).

11. **Pass on concise, clear messages.** When giving messages to colleagues, for example, make sure that you include your name and the date. When messages are unclear or anonymous, time is wasted by people trying to work out what they mean and where they came from, and the paperwork mountain builds faster.

12. **Use sticky notes.** It's useful to have a supply of Post-its or other sticky notes in different colours – even the very smallest ones are useful as an aid for identifying particular papers or pages quickly. Also, scribbling a note on a Post-it is much quicker than typing a memo to accompany a document on its way to a colleague (and it saves trees).

13. **Try to do a paper-sort towards the end of each working day.** Getting rid of the debris, and collecting together papers that need to stay together, are both useful tasks that may not be so easy next day when someone may have tidied your desk up for you! It can be refreshing to see some of the wood of your desktop before you leave at the end of the day.

14. **Don't write too much!** Make your own contributions to the paper mountain as to-the-point and readable as possible, so that people don't have to waste time going through all sorts of background information before coming to the important points you're making.

Chapter 6
Personal and professional development

This chapter is intended for colleagues in libraries who are looking at their career prospects in the profession, rather than just looking for ways to make their day-to-day work more productive and efficient. We start with 'Using conferences for networking'. Working in a service profession, it is all too easy to become preoccupied by the problems and conditions relating to your own particular job, and not to have the opportunity to step back and look at what you do in a more detached way. Participating in conferences can be a remedy for this situation, and we hope our suggestions will help librarians to make the most of such opportunities as they may get to make valuable contacts outside their own working environment. We next offer some suggestions for those brave enough to offer to make contributions to conferences, and who may feel somewhat daunted by the prospect of having to stand up and talk about their work and ideas.

We next turn our attention to the less-public side of professional development. We offer some suggestions about ways to create and maintain your own CV, so that it will serve you as a good ambassador when you may wish to apply for new posts, or for promotion in your own institution. This leads us naturally on to another related topic: 'Giving better interviews'. There will be times when you need to make the impression that you want to on panels of people who don't know how well you work, and our suggestions should help you to put your best foot foremost in such situations.

We end this chapter with two sets of suggestions on performance reviews. Appraisal systems are implemented in many academic institutions, and extend to library staff as well as to academics. Appraisal should ideally be a formative and useful process, concentrating on progression rather than allocating blame for things that are not working well. Therefore, we have made suggestions to people on both sides of the process: appraisers as well as appraisees. Indeed, in many appraisal systems, most people will be involved in both sides of the appraisal equation.

29 Using conferences for networking

Conferences are a good way of getting to know about new developments in your field but, more importantly, they are also invaluable in helping you to get to know other people in your own professional area, giving you a chance to put faces to names you have read about and to broaden your network of contacts. The tips that follow are designed to help you make the most of such occasions.

1. **Go equipped.** If you are in a hall of residence, a good conference kit includes a few tea bags or coffee, a mug, a towel (not always supplied in residences), a dressing gown (unless you are en suite) and a bottle opener (to facilitate after session discussions). You may also like to think about ear plugs, an alarm clock, and a radio.

2. **Find out who is there.** Networking is most successful if you can find someone from another organization where you know something is going on. Read the guest list and work out whom you want to meet.

3. **Ask your own colleagues at work for contacts and requests for information.** Follow up by trying to meet their contacts at the conference. Use their requests for information as part of your agenda for finding out from people at the conference. If your colleagues see that you are doing a good job for everyone by attending a conference, your chances of being asked to go to future conferences will increase.

4. **Leave your mark.** It's a good idea to take a supply of business cards so you can exchange them, and if people offer to send out post-conference information, you can just give them

your card rather than laboriously writing out your name. Self-adhesive small address labels may also be useful, for example, when you want to pass on your home address you can paste one onto the back of a college card.

5. **Wear your badge if one is supplied.** People are more likely to remember who you are for future contact if you are identifiable, and it also makes it easier to generate an air of informality in workshops and seminars if names can be used. It is said that names are remembered better when badges are stuck to the right-hand side of your clothing, so that people see the badge as your right arm is extended to shake hands on first meeting.

6. **Choose your sessions strategically.** Look at the conference programme in advance of arrival if possible so you can make informed choices, rather than signing up for anything at the last minute. Follow your own interests, but also try to go to a couple of sessions that are completely divergent from your own area, to broaden your experience. The sessions with the catchiest titles are not always the most exciting.

7. **Beware of long, parallel sessions!** Sometimes conference programmes include parallel streams, with sessions of different lengths running concurrently. When you are in doubt about what to attend it's safer to choose to go to three short sessions than one long one, in case you find yourself stuck in a long boring one with no easy way of escaping politely!

8. **Pace yourself.** Don't try to go to absolutely everything if it's a packed schedule. You can only take in so much during a conference and it is often better to sit out a session or two (or go for a snooze) than to try to cram everything in.

9. **Don't mix people and papers.** At a conference you will normally collect all sorts of pieces of paperwork: handouts, fliers, and so on. You also are likely to collect people's names,

addresses, or your own notes about people's ideas. It's best to keep the 'people' information out of danger of getting buried in the growing folder of paperwork. A separate envelope or wallet helps you do this.

10. **Take a break!** Many delegates to conferences find that the most valuable things they get out of the event are chats over tea or coffee or meals. Indeed, there are often impromptu huddles of delegates skipping sessions entirely to talk about things of mutual interest. Try to meet as many delegates as you can, and start to build up a network of colleagues who share your interests.

11. **Share out the sessions.** If you're attending a conference with one or more colleagues from your own institution, it can be worth mapping out who will be going to which sessions, so that you between you gather more of what's on offer. Of course, don't miss a key session that you're both (or all) really keen to attend.

12. **File the conference.** You'll probably come back with a file of paperwork, maybe in a conference wallet or folder. Make sure it's labelled with the date, and file it sensibly. Before this, however, take out and act on those pieces of paper you marked for action after the conference: don't file them away forever in the wallet.

13. **Don't leave early!** The final plenary session can be the most important one, even when some delegates have already left. Not only can the session be a good one, but also many useful exchanges of names/addresses and interests can occur after the conference ends, on the way to the station or car park, or over a post-conference drink.

30 Giving presentations at conferences

Making a presentation at a conference can be very rewarding, but it can also feel like an ordeal, particularly if you're new to presenting in this way. We trust that the suggestions below will help to minimize any anxieties you have about making conference presentations, and help you to make effective ones.

1. **Be self-sufficient** If you are doing a workshop or a seminar, take everything you are likely to need with you, such as overhead transparencies (those you've prepared for your presentation and blanks for exercises) pens for OHTs and flipcharts, Blu-Tack, masking tape, scissors, Post-its, and so on, even if all such things you require have been promised by the organizers.

2. **Don't over-rely on IT kit.** If your presentation involves computers, videos or anything sophisticated, have a backup plan of what you could still do if the equipment were to fail at the last minute.

3. **Decide what your audience is meant to get out of your presentation.** It's worth stating your intentions right at the start, maybe as objectives or intended outcomes. When your audience knows what you're trying to do, you'll have less trouble achieving it.

4. **Prepare useful handout material.** The handouts don't have to be very extensive. All you need is a useful digest of the main points from your session. Take plenty of copies of your handout. Even if your session is only to a small audience in a parallel stream, a pile of additional handouts placed on the

conference desk after your session has been given will soon disappear.

5. **Let your handouts help you to make contacts.** Make sure that the handout materials have your name and full address on them, and consider putting in telephone, fax and e-mail details too.

6. **Watch your timing.** No-one likes the conference presenter who overruns. Audiences like there to be time to ask questions too. A good rule of thumb is to prepare to present for only half of the total time allocated to your session, and devote the rest to questions and discussion. However, have a few 'encores' up your sleeve, so that if there is an awkward silence when you open up for questions, you can give some additional presentation as needed.

7. **Use your chairperson, if there is one.** Have a few well chosen words, in clear big print, which you can pass to a chairperson if necessary so you can be introduced effectively. Alternatively, be prepared to say a few words about yourself as you begin (but audiences don't like extensive autobiographies). Don't depend on your chairperson to keep you to time: look after this yourself.

8. **Try to involve your audience.** Even simple things like asking for a show of hands from the audience regarding 'who has had this sort of problem?' can help to make audiences feel involved. Think of ways of getting contributions in writing from each member of your audience (for example, on Post-its). This gives everyone a chance, and avoids over-contribution from irritating know-alls!

9. **Come to a resounding conclusion!** Don't just stop dead. Think carefully how you're going to round off your session, and whether to do this right at the end, or to sum up before opening the session up for questions. Watch how some pre-

senters manage to get rounds of applause: it's usually linked to them having made a final point decisively.

10. **Learn from experience.** After your presentation, jot down two things that you feel worked well, and two suggestions to yourself regarding your next presentation. Also learn by comparing the ways that different presenters succeed, or fail!

31 Creating and maintaining your CV

Every librarian will need a good CV from time to time, whether for applying for jobs, or for promotion, or for other purposes. These suggestions aim to make the task of producing one at short notice less of a hassle.

1. **Collect your data.** It's surprisingly easy to forget important details like dates of qualifications and precise titles of courses you've attended. Make a start on producing a comprehensive CV by checking out and listing accurately all your data.

2. **Make it easy for you to update.** Keep it all on disk in a place where you won't forget it, and date the version you are working on. You can then easily update it and reframe it for different contexts. Save it every time by date, for example as 'CV Chris 13.12.97' (depending on your software) and don't delete older versions as they may often have in them information you've discarded but could want to use again in another context.

3. **Keep several versions of your CV.** You may find you need different versions for different contexts, some perhaps than emphasize your academic qualifications, others that highlight your professional experience. Don't regard your first draft of a CV as universally applicable.

4. **Think about the order of your material.** People often automatically put qualifications and work experience in chronological order, but as you get more experienced it probably looks more impressive to list most recent data first, or to write an executive summary of the main parts.

5. **Think about the visual impact of your CV.** There's no second chance to make a good first impression. A well set out CV on good quality paper, which highlights your best aspects, should make an excellent first impression. Such impressions are often the enduring ones.

6. **Make your CV timeless.** Put in date of birth rather than your age, as this date won't change. Be careful with terms like 'currently' or 'this year' or 'at present'.

7. **Make a habit of regularly reviewing your CV.** It is not uncommon to need a CV at very short notice. This is easier to provide if you have been meticulous about adding achievements, training courses, publications and responsibilities as these occur, rather than leaving it until you need a CV. At such times, you will be working under pressure anyway to get your application in, so having a ready CV is a bonus.

8. **Ask a good friend to look at it carefully.** Someone else can often see the flaws in a CV more easily than the originator. Ask your friend to be critical about unexplained gaps, dates that don't add up, and incomplete information. It's better to get an ally to do this than to wait for a critical reaction from a potential employer, or an awkward interview question that makes you wish you'd been clearer in the information you'd supplied.

9. **Proof read your CV meticulously.** Nothing lets a CV down more than wrongly-spelled words and typographical errors. They give a poor impression of you, and make it look as though you can't even use a spellcheck program.

10. **Don't include irrelevant material.** People producing their first CVs when they have as yet few qualifications and little experience tend to include information about hobbies and leisure pursuits, but once you have plenty to write, don't feel

you still need to include lots of waffle. The art of a good CV is to be succinct, informative, and presentable.

32   Giving better interviews

It can be difficult to make a good impression at interviews, especially if you feel nervous, and really want the job. These tips are designed to help you come across well, even in the most trying circumstances.

1.   **Do your preparation.** Read the advert, the job description, and any supporting documentation that is offered about the job. Make sure that you know exactly what kind of post is on offer, and what kind of person they seem to be looking for.

2.   **Read your own application.** Look at it critically and ask yourself how you match up to their requirements. Look for evidence from your own experience, to offer in support of your claims to be the right person for the job.

3.   **Prepare a list of potential questions which they might ask you.** Many universities and colleges with good equal opportunities policies will set questions based on the published job description and person specification. It should therefore be relatively straightforward to second-guess the kinds of questions that they are likely to ask you.

4.   **Prepare answers to the likely questions.** If, for example, the job requires good interpersonal communications skills, list contexts in which you have demonstrated these, perhaps in dealing with user enquiries, helping to induct new staff, or working on the issue desk.

5.   **Prepare your own questions.** Even if the answers to these have all been covered by the time they ask if you have any questions, if you have some prepared you can at least confirm to them that they have all been covered. It's best to always

have *something* yet to ask, however, something non-controversial!

6. **Put on a good show when being shown around.** Interview candidates are usually shown around the library either before or after interview. The opinions that the staff showing you round form about you may well be important, and worth investing in carefully.

7. **Try to adopt an open posture in interviews.** If your body is hunched or tense, you will convey nervousness and will look unconfident (you will probably feel it too!). Try to sit squarely in your chair, with relaxed hands, and look the questioners clearly in the eyes when responding to questions. This way, you will come across as being open and trustworthy. Don't forget to smile (but not to grin maniacally!).

8. **Be giving in your answers.** Try not to answer in monosyllables, even when they ask you closed questions. Give as full an answer as you can to each question, looking for signs that you have given enough and that they want to continue to ask you further questions.

9. **Listen carefully for the secondary questions.** These are often more probing than the questions the interviewers have on their list, and answering these can give you the chance to shine and be original. Use them as an opportunity to bring your good qualities to the fore and to demonstrate your special suitability for the post.

10. **Watch the interviewers' body language.** You will usually be able to tell from their reactions whether they want you to say more, or whether they are bored silly with your views on cataloguing systems. If they try to shut you up, don't continue, and try not to interrupt their questions or comments, even though you may be bursting to say more.

11. **Retain a sense of proportion.** Many people underperform in interviews because they are nervous. Try to be as relaxed as you can. In the end, it's only a job interview, not a matter of life or death.

33 Preparing for performance reviews

Many institutions will have their own systems for the appraisal of employees' performance, and there is often training or guidance for the appraisers and appraisees alike. Where there is no training, the following suggestions may be helpful in setting an agenda for performance review.

Appraisers

1. **Set an agenda with the appraisee before the occasion itself.** Involve the appraisee in listing the areas that are likely to arise in the interview, so that preparation can be done and evidence of achievement be accumulated.

2. **Allow sufficient time for the review.** Don't assume that you can cram a performance review in between meetings, as appraising performance can be a lengthy process. Try to agree in advance with your appraisee how long the occasion will last, and be flexible if it turns out that more time is needed.

3. **Make proper arrangements for reviews.** Ensure that they take place in a context where you will not be interrupted by people or telephones. Let colleagues know that you do not want to be disturbed.

4. **Make the context welcoming.** Offer tea or coffee to the appraisee if possible, and avoid seating arrangements that reflect the power differential between the two of you, such as the appraisee sitting in front of your desk with you sitting behind it.

5. **Confirm the agenda with the appraisee.** Make sure that you both agree on the scope of the review, on the approximate time scale for the occasion, and on what kinds of outcomes are likely to be the results of your discussions.

6. **Let the appraisee do most of the talking.** The role of the appraiser will usually be to prompt the appraisee into constructive self-review, monitoring performance against goals and targets.

7. **Make the focus of appraisal developmental.** It should not be an occasion for going over old ground or attributing blame for failure. Concentrate on the positive, on achievements and successes, without ignoring problematic areas. These should be the focus for forward planning for improvement.

8. **Performance reviews should lead forward as well as look back.** At least part of the time should be kept available for action planning and goal setting. Try to set 'SMART' targets: specific, measurable, achievable, realistic, and time-contingent.

9. **Offer support.** When you are a budget holder, review how you can support all of your appraisees in terms of their development and training. Remember however, that there may be low-cost solutions you may also consider, such as work-shadowing and task exchanges.

10. **Be as good as your word.** If you have suggested that you will explore funding for specialist training, don't let this slip to the back of your mind, or the appraisee will lose confidence in the whole process. If it turns out that you can't do what you had hoped to do, explain this to the appraisee, with reasons, and if possible look for alternative courses of action to your original plan.

Appraisees

1. **Prepare thoughtfully for your review.** Try to ensure that you have a clear idea before the review of the areas you aim to focus on.

2. **Try to see both sides of the process.** If you're preparing for review, think about how it feels to be in your position, so that when (now or later) people will be preparing to be reviewed by you, you will be as understanding and helpful to them as you can.

3. **Collect evidence of achievement.** Bring to the review, or make a list of, concrete examples of outcomes that you have achieved, so that any successes or progress you claim can be backed up with examples.

4. **Regard the review as an opportunity.** Make it an occasion where you can raise all the important issues you haven't had time to discuss earlier. Have a mental shopping list of training you would like agreement that you can undertake, or aspects of your job description that you would like to develop.

5. **Review your own performance objectively.** Don't over-claim success, or down-grade your own achievements. Try to analyse what has gone well, and why, as well as what has been less successful, and why.

6. **Don't hide your light under a bushel.** Without being boastful, you can use appraisal as an opportunity to celebrate the things you are proud of. Often people are not fully aware of what individuals have done, and how much of a cooperative activity has in fact been the responsibility of one person. Don't be shy about blowing your own trumpet. Such chances don't come very often!

7. **Be realistic about your part in areas that have not been successes.** There's no need to shoulder all the blame, but the performance review is a chance to analyse how much responsibility you bear for the projects that have not succeeded, or for the deadlines that have been missed. This is the time for you to learn from the mistakes of the past and look forward to the next era.

8. **Be clear about the outcomes you would like from your performance review.** If there is training you feel you need to help you do your job properly, or equipment or other resources, then speak out. You may not get everything you want, but you stand a better chance if you discuss it than if you wait silently in hope.

9. **Write your own private reflective log after your appraisal.** This can include how you felt when discussing your successes or failures, and notes to yourself about how you will go about following up your commitments arising from the review.

10. **Remember that appraisal is a process and not an event.** Don't regard the date of your appraisal interview as the be-all and end-all of appraisal. It may be quite a crucial date, but it is only a milestone on a continuing journey.

Chapter 7
Putting training to work

Our final chapter focuses on various aspects of training. The suggestions in this chapter are primarily aimed at those taking responsibility for planning, arranging, or delivering training events for staff in libraries, but should also be of interest to anyone being trained in such events, not least with regard to determining their own targets from such training.

Our first three sets of suggestions are about planning and running training days, starting with the matter of 'Taking responsibility for training' – which can be a thankless task at times. We then consider the practicalities of planning and running training days.

We end this chapter with sets of suggestions which relate specifically to the different training environments involved in large-group events, small group training sessions, and one-to-one training.

The actual agendas for training programmes can be very wide, and can relate to almost every heading in the other chapters in this book, and to many further topics and themes. We hope, however, that the suggestions we have made about the processes of effective training will be able to be translated or adapted to each specific need and occasion.

34 Taking responsibility for training

In many libraries, the responsibility for training falls to one person who then has the task of devising and running a training programme for a whole team. This is often seen as one of the worst jobs in the entire library unless training is seen as a group responsibility. It is one of the least sought-after jobs, but one of the most important. Tips in following sections will help you actually to run the sessions for your colleagues and for other library users, but often some guidance is needed on *what* to run training on as well as how to do it. This section may help.

1. **Try to overcome the feeling that training is a bolt-on chore.** Training works best when it is something that people look forward to, and this feeling is promoted when training sessions provide a constant flow of new ideas, most of which are derived from the participants themselves, rather than being imposed on them by a trainer.

2. **Rotate the responsibility for training.** Unexpected talents can be discovered when training sessions are devised and run by a wide range of the staff of the library, rather than just senior personnel or outside trainers.

3. **Brainstorm with your team what training needs you have collectively.** Get everyone to pitch in with ideas and don't censor seemingly daft ideas at this early stage. Aim for lots of ideas and get people to build on one another's. Flip chart the ideas as they are generated or build a graffiti wall with post-its that can be grouped into clusters of similar ones.

4. **Think about when it will be best to undertake the training.** It may be possible to close the whole library for a short period to enable staff training to take place. It is then important to be able to demonstrate to the rest of the community that there are positive benefits from this exercise.

5. **Try to involve all members of staff.** It is too easy for staff training sessions to be taken over by senior staff or subject librarians, and for junior staff and library assistants to feel that they have little to contribute. Ensure that not all of the training sessions will be solely pitched at the needs of professional staff.

6. **Prioritize the most important themes for training.** Get your colleagues to identify which for them are the most important areas for training, either by a voting system or simply by asterisking the ones that are a high priority for them.

7. **Identify exactly what the intended learning outcomes will be.** This helps to ensure that training is successful and relevant. It also helps you work out the timescales of training programmes, and the group size that is most suitable for the topics to be covered. After a training element is completed, check whether these outcomes have actually been achieved in practice.

8. **Ensure that the training is relevant to the library.** There are many enjoyable training videos available, but these are often seen primarily as entertainment simply because they may have been designed for the business or retail community rather than for librarians. Such resources can still be used effectively if you add some group work before and after the viewing, linking the matters arising from the materials to the everyday running of the library.

9. **Decide who will do the training.** Some of the topics on your list will be in your own area of expertise, others could be facilitated by members of the team, but for some you will need to bring in outside expertise.

10. **Justify the importance of your training programmes.** Staff training can be the one time in the week (or the year) when nearly all of your staff are together, and this in itself is particularly valuable in large libraries. Check that the time will be well spent. Make sure that the 'news round' which often starts off large get-togethers is handled efficiently, and does not eat too much into the time for training.

11. **Obtain a training budget.** This need not be substantial. A little cash to bring in outside experts, to provide refreshments or specialist equipment or materials, or to enable training to take place off-site can sometimes make a great deal of difference to a training programme.

12. **Set aside regular times for training.** It's easy to let training slip off the agenda unless there is a programme of activities. Ideally use times when a whole team of people can undertake training together, perhaps when the library is closed to the public. Regular small scale sessions can often have greater effect than whole days or weekends at a stretch.

13. **Think laterally about training.** Training doesn't always have to involve courses or formal sessions. Often the best kinds of training involve shadowing someone else's work practice, learning by doing or exchanging tasks for periods of time.

14. **Investigate the availability of technological support.** Frequently packages are available on CD-ROM or online for training in all kinds of fields. Don't disregard the potential of older technologies like video and audio tapes, which can be

invaluable in training about interpersonal activities such as making meetings more effective or writing reports.

15. **Think about collaborative training.** Look at exchanging expertise with colleagues in other local universities and other sectors. It can often be more cost-effective to run joint sessions, which can also provide useful networking opportunities.

16. **Try to anticipate training needs.** When moving towards major changes, it is useful if you can gather from colleagues ideas on the things they may need help with. This helps to ensure that training provision will be relevant, and that colleagues will have a sense of ownership of the training programme and processes.

35 Planning a staff training programme

Effective, relevant training not only increases the quality of the ways that a good library operates, but it also enhances the job satisfaction of everyone working there. Training programmes are also opportunities to get people together, and to help them to work together well. The following suggestions will help you to plan an effective programme.

1. **Keep abreast of what's happening elsewhere.** Find out from colleagues in other institutions what sorts of courses, workshops, and learning packages are in use for library staff there. Find out too what they think of each different component of the training provision.

2. **Keep track of the staff training that goes on in your own institution.** Especially if your institution operates at a number of sites it is probable that there will be relevant staff training events you could consider going to yourself, or bringing to your own site. It is useful to be involved in any regional library training groups, and to have an active staff training group at your own site.

3. **Nominate someone to act as the coordinator for suggestions for staff training.** Set up a mechanism for recording training needs that arise in everyday situations.

4. **Get everyone together and brainstorm training needs ideas.** A productive way is to ask everyone to write down completions of the phrase: 'Things would be much better if only I...'. Many of the responses to this sentence-start can be identified as potential training needs.

5. **Prioritize shared training needs.** Put colleagues into groups of four or five, and ask each group to prepare a flipchart listing the training needs they've identified, in order of priority. When several groups' charts have similar topics in the top few places, you can be sure that it will be worth looking hard at how best to get some training on these topics in place as soon as possible.

6. **Get groups thinking about the possible processes.** For example, if colleagues have selected the theme of 'time management' as a shared training need, get them thinking about how best to approach providing such training. Get them to work out the advantages and disadvantages of (for example) a half-day workshop with an external facilitator, an in-house training session, sending people on relevant courses, or buying in training packages, and so on.

7. **Turn training needs into intended outcomes.** Get colleagues thinking about exactly what they would like to be able to demonstrate at the end of a successful episode of training. Often, working out the exact intended outcomes helps a lot in deciding which sorts of training provision will work best.

8. **Make sure everyone is trained in something!** Training is an investment in people, and people feel bad if they're not being invested in. Spread the training budget around, so that everyone has opportunities to have some training .

9. **Draw up an overall training programme and strategy.** You are more likely to be able to secure funding for future training if you can demonstrate convincingly and clearly how you are spending whatever you already have. Seek comments and advice on your strategy from colleagues in personnel or educational development.

10. **Build in flexibility.** It's worth planning some of the training sessions without an advance agenda. Having now and then a half-day set aside in advance, where a team can meet and discuss 'matters arising' on a topical issue, is a useful part of any training strategy.

11. **Consider awaydays.** It does a lot to bring colleagues together, and makes them feel more valued, if sometimes training events can be held in attractive or comfortable surroundings away from the institution. Good catering helps even more!

12. **Plan training evaluation right from the start.** Continuously monitoring the effectiveness of each increment of training allows you to build up a picture of what works well, and what to avoid in future planning. Also, you'll need evaluation evidence to help you to justify how your training budget has been spent and in your bids for future funding for training.

36   Running a staff training day

Effective, productive and happy staff training days don't just happen, they are the end result of careful planning. The following guidelines may help librarians to avoid some of the things that can go wrong.

1. **Plan the day well in advance.** Make sure that everyone who needs to be there will be available, taking into account leave, holidays, and everything that can be anticipated. Ensure that the day is marked in everyone's diary.

2. **Publicize your training day well.** Make sure that publicity is not just adequate, but interesting, and make it clearly relevant to all your intended participants.

3. **Work out 'sharp' intended outcomes for the day.** Keep them reasonable and achievable. Make sure that they're what people really *want* from the day, and what they really *need* from the day as well.

4. **Decide who's going to run the day.** You may be able to choose from various possibilities, including outside consultants, other colleagues in your institution's training or educational development sections, or someone from your own library. Whoever is to be involved, liaise carefully with them from the outset, and allow them to help you to adjust or extend the intended outcomes for the day.

5. **Check out visiting trainers' credibility.** Use your contacts in other institutions to check out that a visiting consultant is of the required calibre and has the appropriate expertise.

6. **Plan the timings.** It's important to have a sensible start-time, so that colleagues don't waste time waiting for latecom-

ers. It's equally important to have a realistic finishing time, so that some colleagues don't have to leave before the end to pick up children from school, for example.

7. **Plan the breaks.** If it's an all-day workshop, you'll need tea/coffee breaks at least once during the morning and the afternoon, and a meal break at lunchtime. It's better to have a 20-minute coffee-break with a punctual re-start, than to try to squeeze in a 10-minute break with a 'slack' re-start. Alternatively, you may be able to combine a break with a group task, where people do the task armed with tea and coffee.

8. **Don't be mean with the refreshments.** It doesn't cost much more to provide biscuits, snacks, scones, cakes, and so on, as well as soft drinks for anyone who doesn't like tea or coffee. Afternoon sessions usually proceed with greater effectiveness if everyone's enjoyed some lunch. Laying on good refreshments helps to keep the whole group together all day, instead of people nipping off during breaks to attend to other business.

9. **Don't bolt the lunch!** In some large, multisite libraries, a training event may be the only time in the year when all staff are together and can actually see one another, rather than just talking on phones or corresponding through e-mail or paper. Occasions when people can talk informally to one another are very valuable, and such an occasion is the lunch break on a training day.

10. **Use humour.** Be as informal as possible, encourage exchanges of experience – both good and bad.

11. **Avoid sexist or racist language or images.** This may seem an unnecessary suggestion, and many people are very careful to avoid giving offence in such ways, but when offence *is* given or taken, the degree of intensity of feelings produced should

not be underestimated. Someone who has been offended in such ways can switch off from everything of value in the training session.

12. **Encourage a supportive, blame-free atmosphere.** Imagine the problems that a staff-training day for academics on 'lecturing' would have if the agenda were to focus too much on 'everything that you do wrong in your lectures!'. Use staff training to start with problems that staff know they have, and look for constructive solutions to these.

13. **Look after the facilitator well.** If an outside consultant is involved, ensure that the person concerned has good travel directions, and make sure that someone is available to meet them at an appropriate place. Check out in advance what facilities may be needed, such as an overhead projector, flipchart or video, and how the chairs and tables should be arranged in the room at the start of the session.

14. **Plan active training events.** People learn more by doing things, discussing them, making decisions, trying out things, and brainstorming ideas, than by listening to someone talking about it 'from the front'. Don't underestimate the time taken for individual or group activities. It's better to have some time left over to do some more of the activity, than to allow the timescale for the day to fall behind owing to tasks over-running.

15. **Use training events to agree next steps.** Getting people together for a training workshop is even more useful when they can use parts of the event to agree an action plan regarding how they may be going to implement things covered in the workshop.

16. **Don't commit yourself to follow up activities unless you really mean it.** It's easy enough to offer to type up and disseminate workshop products in the heat of the moment,

but it can be a real chore when you're actually doing it. Only offer to undertake this if you can see real benefit in doing so.

17. **Use a good room.** A dark cubby-hole with no natural lighting and grubby furniture may be OK for the occasional meeting but will spell disaster for a training session for a whole day. Use the best possible room available, which doesn't have to be plush, but should be well ventilated and lit with appropriate facilities.

18. **Try to get the temperature right!** It's sometimes hard to please everyone, but either extremes of temperature are likely to be very destructive regarding your training day. People who are too cold become depressed or rebellious, and people who are too warm can be sluggish and easily bored. Where possible, have some control of the heating so that different parts of your venue can be adjusted to suit particular participants' needs and wishes.

19. **Think about room layout.** If you want staff to interact with one another, don't sit them in serried ranks. If you want them to look at a lot of documents, don't sit them in a friendly table-less ring with nowhere to put their papers.

20. **Organize the kit.** It's a nightmare if people want to use PowerPoint and you've only provided a conventional OHP, and even traditionalists need one with a functioning bulb in it! Check out presenters' requirements for audiovisual equipment, IT kit, and low-tech equipment such as flip chart paper and Blu-tack. Don't forget to check the kit out on the day and make sure that there are no last-minute problems.

21. **Make the participants work.** Don't feel that you have to do all the presentation. If you recognize the expertise of the participants and build upon it in your sessions, you will soon get a reputation as a wise and knowledgeable facilitator.

22. **Vary the activities.** Participants get tired of continuous presentations, but they also get bored with an endless cycle of group tasks with flipchart, followed by report backs and plenaries. Keep them busy, keep them active, keep them guessing!

23. **Be prepared for people coming and going.** It can be intensely annoying when people arrive late, disappear early and slip out in the middle, but workshop organizers have to recognize that participants often have other commitments running alongside the workshop, so be tolerant of their behaviour.

24. **Agree groundrules for the session.** People will need to know what level of confidentiality is present in the discussions before they get involved in many kinds of discussions. A lot of the problems of lack of participation in workshops or over-dominance by one or two individuals can be avoided if expectations are made clear from the start.

25. **Have contingency plans for when things go wrong.** If you have prepared a structured day around group activities, be ready for there to be insufficient people to run the group tasks as planned, or for the room layout to be inflexible or for things to overrun, particularly if you are new to the game. Don't make everything rely on IT or audiovisual equipment being available and working.

26. **Pace yourself.** Running training events can be exhausting, so make use of the time when participants are on a task to catch your breath, gather your wits and prepare yourself for the next section of the programme. Don't feel you have to run round monitoring their activities: they'll probably get more done without you being there.

27. **Always make time to gather feedback.** It's only too easy for workshops to overrun, and the vital matter of getting par-

ticipants' feedback to be forgotten. It's useful to have a short questionnaire for everyone to fill in at the end of a session, and not to accept 'I'll send it in later' as an excuse for not doing this. If 'considered' feedback is wanted, a separate later questionnaire is best, including specific questions about how useful the content of the training event turned out to be in practice.

37 Training with large groups

You may already be comfortable running training sessions for large groups of people, whether it involves large student groups, or even large groups of library staff. For many people, starting to run large-group training sessions can be somewhat frightening, and the suggestions below are intended to help such people tackle the job constructively and systematically.

1. **Check out the venue.** Get the feel of the place you are working in by visiting the room where you will be training and practising speaking and using the equipment before anyone else arrives.

2. **Speak up.** Lots of people feel very nervous about speaking in public because they worry about their voices. Take a friend along to the practice session and check out whether you are audible. If you are not, take deeper breaths to help your voice project further, slow down a little and articulate (that is move your mouth to make the speech sounds) just a little more strongly.

3. **Make sure that everyone can see.** Check that your overheads or flipcharts can be read clearly from all parts of the room, and that the furniture is not arranged in ways that cause blind spots. With large groups, keep the wording on overheads or flipcharts to a minimum, and use font sizes of at least 18 point if you are using a wordprocessing package.

4. **Use any nervousness to energize.** It's actually much better to be a little nervous, and let that come across as intensity of dedication to the task you are doing, than to appear too laid-back and blasé.

5. **Don't believe that everyone will see your mistakes!** In practice, no-one working with large groups has their undivided attention for very long, which means that when you make a slip, most people will not even notice it.

6. **Structure your session.** It's particularly important to make clear at the outset what the intended learning outcomes are for the session. If your participants know where they are heading, and why they are heading there, they are more likely to be receptive to the ideas you bring to the session.

7. **Give them something to look at.** If you feel self-conscious when a sea of eyes is looking at you, turn their attention to the overhead projector, a handout or a wallboard. This can give you time to regain your composure, adjust your clothing, sneeze, or find the overhead you want to show next!

8. **Give them things to do.** Even when working with large groups, you can get everyone in the room participating. For example, ask them key questions, about which to write their individual replies in a few words on Post-its, then stick them to the walls and compare notes.

9. **Give them chances to talk back.** Most people enjoy airing their views, ideas and opinions, and they often remember these parts of a large-group session rather better than what was said by the presenter. Be careful to ensure that one or two vociferous participants don't dominate things too much: open up matters arising for everyone else to think about and to join in with their contributions.

10. **Give them a break.** Tea and coffee breaks are important to participants, and it's important to take such breaks punctually!

38   Training in small groups

Training is often carried out in groups of up to eight or so participants. This may not feel as daunting as working with a large group in a lecture theatre but can still be pretty intimidating for the person who is not used to working in this way. These tips are designed to take some of the heat out of the situation for novices and to provide a few new ideas for the old hands.

1.   **Learn everyone's names.** People respond so much better if you can speak to them personally in small group training. Even if you have a poor memory, you should strive to call ·people by name in a small group session. Get them to use badges or name cards, or use a seating plan if you find difficulties.

2.   **Check that everyone can see and hear.** It's easy to forget that a monitor can be difficult to see even if only three or four are grouped round it. Watch out for extraneous noise (printers, for example) that make it difficult for people to hear you.

3.   **Consider the different levels of ability in the group.** In any session, you are likely to find a wide diversity of experience and ability. It's difficult to cope with those who are very slow on the uptake at the same time as those who take to your material very readily. It often helps to have a set of 'headlines' for your training, that is, the central points carrying the basic information. You can elaborate on these for the more able as you go along.

4.   **Provide differentiated tasks so people can work at their own pace.** Inevitably people will work at different rates in group sessions, so it is helpful to have a range of tasks of vary-

ing difficulty, so that those who are racing away don't get frustrated by being held back by the plodders.

5. **Try to ensure there is fair turn taking.** Bossy, needy or self-important people often monopolize training sessions. It can be difficult if the status of the participants at a training session is very different, because those on lower scales may feel unable to interrupt the more senior people.

6. **Be aware that peer pressure might make people afraid to admit their incompetence.** In mixed sessions, people may be nervous about showing themselves up in front of others, so may hesitate to ask questions or join in.

7. **Balance presentation with individual activity.** Concentration levels fall fast if people are expected to sit and listen to a trainer for too long. The essence of training is helping people to get to grips with practical activities, so let them do it, while at the same time giving them sufficient input from you to give them confidence.

8. **Make time for questions.** Don't just leave it to the end, give your participants lots of opportunities to check their own understanding and sort out any problems. Often people learn more from getting their queries sorted out than from any other part of the training session.

9. **Keep to time within the session.** This means having a structure in mind that is flexible enough to cope with interruptions and problems, and trying to ensure that you stick reasonably closely to it.

10. **Finish well.** Try to ensure that the session doesn't just tail off, even if the second half has involved individual work. Call the group together and provide closure to the session by summarizing key learning points, advising participants where to get further help and getting feedback.

39 Training on a one-to-one basis

Academic librarians are frequently called upon to undertake individual training in all kinds of contexts. A lot of training is quite informal, a common style being 'sitting with Nelly', that is, working alongside someone to help them get the hang of things. However, one-to-one training can be a really important part of a training programme if it is undertaken systematically and with tact.

1. **Allow yourself time to prepare.** It's easy to think that when you are training only one person you can do it 'off the cuff', but it usually works best if you prepare as carefully as you would for training a group. Even with quite a short session it's a good idea to have clear objectives and a plan of what is to be achieved within the time available.

2. **Set the parameters at the beginning of the session.** It's not always clear in one-to-one work when the session moves from a welcoming chat to the actual training. Check out how much time is available and what constraints there are.

3. **Clarify what prior knowledge and experience the trainee has.** This will give you a starting point for your training. Try to find out what are the needs of your trainee. This may not be easy as s/he may not know what they are, and often the 'presenting problem' is not the most important one.

4. **Let the trainee set the pace.** Try not to dazzle them with jargon and move just a step at a time. Listen to queries and answer them to the trainee's satisfaction. Don't try to cover too much if the trainee is finding it heavy going. Never give them too much information at once that they can't easily assimilate.

5. **Help them to learn by doing.** Keep your own hands off the keyboard and talk them through the different stages rather than doing things for them. It can be terribly frustrating waiting for people to find their way through what seem to you like simple procedures, but your trainees will become disempowered if you keep reaching across and doing it for them.

6. **Think about personal space.** Your physical position in relation to the trainee is important, because some people feel very uncomfortable when very close to others. It's probably easiest, for example, when working together on a computer to sit just to the side of and slightly behind the trainee. Avoid standing too close behind the trainee or making anyone uncomfortable by guiding their hand without permission.

7. **Allow for different learning styles.** Some people can remember oral instructions easily, others feel much more confident if they write down everything you tell them. Some like to work from preprinted handouts, others prefer their own shorthand notes and diagrams.

8. **Watch your language!** Avoid jargon at all costs and remember that terms, acronyms and key words that are second nature to you might be a foreign language to a newcomer.

9. **Respect the trainee.** Often people feel very foolish if they can't access the information they want or can't perform pretty basic IT tasks. Try not to let them feel foolish and never put students down or scoff at their incompetence.

10. **Finish the session cleanly.** Make it quite clear when the session is finished and give the trainee an idea of what will happen next, whether further sessions will follow and whether individual work is needed before the next session. Provide opportunities for the trainee to give you feedback on the session so that you can continuously improve.

Conclusions

This is only the first edition of *500 tips for academic librarians*. We hope that you have found in it some suggestions which you can use straightaway, as well as some which you can aim to implement when conditions allow you to do so. We also hope that you will have taken pride in all the suggestions we have made that you have already achieved and exceeded, and that you will not have felt patronized by our comments relating to all those things that you are already doing well.

However, in a book of this sort, we are not so vain as to think that we have addressed everything that could possibly help colleagues working in academic library environments. We will be delighted to receive feedback from *you*, through Library Association Publishing, which will help us to make the next edition of our book better.

Please write on the form below, and forward it to our publishers.

What did you like best about this book?

What did you like least about this book?

Which suggestions did you find most useful?

Which of our suggestions did you think were just not on!

Which areas did you feel we may have missed altogether?

Any other comments? Please feel free to send more than just this form.

Your name and address:

As is our practice, all useful suggestions will be gratefully acknowledged in our next edition.

Further reading

We have listed below some books which may be useful sources for further reading, following on from some of the themes addressed in the current volume.

Armstrong, S., Thompson, G. and Brown, S. (eds.), *Facing up to radical change in universities*, Kogan Page, London, 1996.

Baker, D. (ed.), *Resource management in academic libraries*, Library Association Publishing, London, 1997.

Biddiscombe R. (ed.), *The end-user revolution*, Library Association Publishing, London, 1996.

Biddiscombe, R. (ed.), *Training for IT*, Library Association Publishing, London, 1997.

Bourner, T. and Race, P., *How to win as a part-time student*, Kogan Page, London, 1994.

Brown, S. and Smith B. (eds.), *Resource-based learning*, Kogan Page, London, 1996.

Brown, S., Race, P. and Smith, B., *500 tips on assessment*, Kogan Page, London, 1996.

Chalmers, D. and Fuller, R., *Teaching for learning at university*, Kogan Page, London, 1996.

Further Education Funding Council, *Inclusive learning: principles and recommendations* (The 'Tomlinson' Report), FEFC, Coventry, UK.

Norman, S. (ed.), *Copyright in further and higher education libraries* (LA Copyright Guide), 3rd edn, Library Association Publishing, London, 1996.

Owen, T,. *Success at the enquiry desk*, rev edn, Library Association Publishing, London, 1996.

Parry, J., *Induction*, Library Association Publishing, London, 1993.

Pinder, C. and Melling, M., *Providing customer-oriented services in academic libraries*, London, Library Association Publishing, 1996.

Further reading

Race, P. and McDowell, S., *500 computing tips for lecturers and teachers*, Kogan Page, London, 1993.

Winship, I. and McNab, A., *The student's guide to the Internet*, London, Library Association Publishing, 1996.

Index

Index